The Complete Guide to Shorkies

Candace Darnforth

LP Media Inc. Publishing
Text copyright © 2020 by LP Media Inc.
All rights reserved.

No part of this book may be reproduced or transmitted in any form or by any means, electronic or mechanical, including photocopying, recording, or by an information storage and retrieval system – except by a reviewer who may quote brief passages in a review to be printed in a magazine or newspaper – without permission in writing from the publisher. For information address LP Media Inc. Publishing, 3178 253rd Ave. NW, Isanti, MN 55040

www.lpmedia.org

Publication Data

Candace Darnforth

The Complete Guide to Shorkies – First edition.

Summary: "Successfully raising a Shorkie Dog from puppy to old age" – Provided by publisher.

ISBN: 978-1-954288-02-7

[1. Shorkies – Non-Fiction] I. Title.

This book has been written with the published intent to provide accurate and authoritative information in regard to the subject matter included. While every reasonable precaution has been taken in preparation of this book the author and publisher expressly disclaim responsibility for any errors, omissions, or adverse effects arising from the use or application of the information contained inside. The techniques and suggestions are to be used at the reader's discretion and are not to be considered a substitute for professional veterinary care. If you suspect a medical problem with your dog, consult your veterinarian.

Design by Sorin Rădulescu

First paperback edition, 2021

Photo Courtesy of Lori Laabs

TABLE OF CONTENTS

INTRODUCTION
Did you just bring home your new Shorkie? ... 1

CHAPTER 1
Meet the Shorkie ... 3
What is a Shorkie? ... 4
What is a Designer or Hybrid Dog? ... 4
History of the Shorkie ... 6
Shih Tzu ... 6
Yorkshire Terrier ... 8
Physical Appearance and Temperament ... 8
Is a Shorkie the Right Fit for You? ... 10

CHAPTER 2
Choosing a Shorkie ... 11
Buying vs. Adopting ... 12
Shelters and Rescues ... 14
How to Find a Reputable Breeder ... 16
Important Questions to Ask the Breeder ... 18
Breeder Contracts and Guarantees ... 20
Male vs. Female ... 21
Picking the Correct Puppy for You ... 21

CHAPTER 3
What to Expect for the First Few Months ... 23
Puppy-Proofing Your Home – Inside and Out ... 24
Shopping List ... 28

Establish Puppy House Rules and Daily Routines 31
The Ride Home 33
The First Day 35
First Night 37
First Vet Visit 37
Obedience Classes 38

CHAPTER 4

Laying a Solid Foundation to Train Your Shorkie **39**
Disobedient or Bad Parenting? 40
How to Teach an Old Dog New Tricks 43
When to Call a Professional 45
Unacceptable Behavior from Day One 46
    Chewing 47
    Excessive Barking 47
    Digging 47
    Separation Anxiety 47
    Running away 48
    Jumping up 48
    Begging 48

CHAPTER 5

Everything You Need to Know About Housetraining **49**
Crate Training Basics 50
How to Crate Train 52
Housetraining Basics 55
    Potty pads vs. Litter box 58
Cleaning up after your Shorkie 61
Rewarding Positive Behavior 61
When to Use a Playpen 62

CHAPTER 6

Socializing Your Shorkie **63**
Why Socialize Your Shorkie? 64

Introducing Your New Puppy to Other Dogs 65
Socializing with Other Pets 67
    Cats and Dogs 68
    Socializing with other animals 69
What if Your Pets Don't Get Along? 70
Shorkies and Strangers 71
Shorkies and Children 73

CHAPTER 7

Puppy-Parenting 75
Common puppy-parenting mistakes 76
How Do You Become the Alpha? 78
Consistency is Fundamental 79
Clicker Training – It Really Works 81
Mental Stimulation 84

CHAPTER 8

Basic Commands 85
Benefits of proper training 86
Picking the Right Rewards/Treats 88
Basic Commands 89
    Sit 91
    Stay 91
    Down 91
    Come 92
    Off 92
    Leave It 93
How to introduce the Leash and Collar 93
Advanced Commands 95
    Look 95
    No 96
    Roll Over 96

CHAPTER 9

Traveling 97
Preparing Your Shorkie for Travel 98
Traveling by Car 100
    The Right Crate for Long Distance Car Travel: 102
Traveling by Plane 103
Lodging Away from Home 106
Kenneling vs. Dog-sitters 107
    Boarding Kennels 107
    Dog-sitter 109

CHAPTER 10

Nutrition 111
Importance of a Wholesome Diet 112
Human Foods to Avoid 113
Commercial Dog Food 115
How to Read Dog Food Labels 118
Making Homemade Dog Food 121
    A Basic Recipe for Homemade Dog Food 122
Weight Monitoring 123

CHAPTER 11

Grooming your Shorkie 125
Brushing 125
Bathing 127
Nail Clipping 128
Importance of Good Dental Care 129
Paws 131
Ears 131
Eyes 132
Professional Grooming 133

CHAPTER 12

Preventive Medical Care ... **135**
Choosing a Veterinarian ... 136
Microchipping ... 136
Neutering and Spaying ... 138
Internal Parasites ... 139
Fleas and Ticks ... 143
Holistic Alternatives to Conventional Veterinary Medicine ... 147
Vaccinations ... 148
Pet insurance ... 150

CHAPTER 13

Caring for a Senior Shorkie ... **151**
Physical and Mental Signs of Aging ... 152
Illness and Injury Prevention ... 154
Common, Age-Related Illnesses ... 156
Grooming ... 157
Nutrition Needs ... 159
    Choosing a Premium Senior Dog Food ... 160
Exercise ... 162
Saying Goodbye ... 164

INTRODUCTION
Did you just bring home your new Shorkie?

Whether you have a new puppy or an older dog, you have now encountered your new best friend, whose only purpose is to warm your heart and enrich the quality of your life, at least for the next ten years or more. Trust me, you have made the best decision ever by letting your new puppy into your life!

Your Shorkie will be by your side through thick and thin, giving you a constant flow of love and affection. Plus, he will give you countless hours of amusement, and you might even find yourself needing to buy a new cell phone with more memory because of all the adorable videos and pictures you will be taking of your new furry friend.

However, the first few months with your dog are essential in establishing what you consider to be acceptable and unacceptable behavior. Nobody wants an uncontrollable dog or even worse, one that is aggressive. The goal

Photo Courtesy of Cynthia Brumer

INTRODUCTION   Did you just bring home your new Shorkie?

of this book is to help you and your family establish a positive relationship with your new dog, right from the very first minute you meet and bring him home.

Photo Courtesy of Steph Whyman

A positive relationship is so much more than just love and affection. It involves many hours of consistent training. If you start training your Shorkie from day one and use the different suggestions in this book, I guarantee you will have an obedient Shorkie who will respect and love you! All dogs are instinctively loyal to their new owners, and they want to please you. However, they need guidance, they need you to teach them, and they are not going learn on their own.

Everything you need to know about training your Shorkie can be found in this book... training, nutrition, grooming, and so much more. The suggestions in this book will help you communicate to your dog what is expected of him in a way that he will actually understand, which will form an unbreakable bond of friendship between the two of you. So, keep reading to embark on a journey with your new best friend!

CHAPTER 1
Meet the Shorkie

The Shorkie is one of the world's most beloved 'designer' dog breeds, and it's not too hard to see why. Shorkies are praised for their affectionate and cheerful personality, as well as their intelligence. They're renowned for making excellent family pets and for quickly adapting to their new family environment, other dogs, pets, and especially children. Many dog owners consider them to be the ultimate house pet.

Shorkies are known for eagerly waiting for their owner to return home; an anticipation filled with compassionate eyes, a wiggly tail, and a cheerful attitude. Their love and energy are extremely contagious and will surely bring a smile to your face in an instant!

They might be small in size, but what they lack in size, they make up for with cuteness and a huge dose of loyalty by inheriting the best qualities from both of their parents.

Photo Courtesy of Levana Burke

CHAPTER 1   Meet the Shorkie

What is a Shorkie?

Shorkies are considered to be a designer breed or a hybrid because they are a cross between two toy-sized purebreds – the Shih Tzu and the Yorkshire Terrier. Often, depending on where you live in the world, they can be called Chorkies, Shih Tzu-Yorkie mix, or Shitzu Yorkie.

> **FUN FACT**
> **A Shorkie By Any Other Name**
>
> Shorkies are a cross between a Shih Tzu and Yorkshire Terrier. While the most popular term for these adorable dogs is "Shorkie," they are also sometimes called Yorkie Tzus, Shorkie Tzus, or Shih Tzu-Yorkies.

Don't let their tiny size fool you! They are known for having a huge personality that will steal the hearts of everyone around them. Even though they are best suited for smaller families or seniors, they also will thrive in a larger family environment. They love going for walks, but their favorite place is to be cuddled up on your lap or by your side. Your Shorkie will have lots of energy and can spend hours upon hours playing fetch, but they can also easily be distracted with a chew toy.

However, I must warn you, their sense of loyalty and the need to protect those they love will make your Shorkie quite yappy. If you don't want a loyal guard dog that yaps at anything that moves, then you will need to spend extra time training him when to bark and when barking is considered to be bad behavior.

What is a Designer or Hybrid Dog?

A purebred dog's genetic pattern is well-established. This means every puppy litter will have a similar temperament, personality, and appearance. One of the main advantages to buying a purebred is you know exactly what type of dog you will be getting. Yet, due to close inter-breeding, the dogs' gene pool can become thin, causing serious genetic defects. For this very reason, many professional breeders have started to cross with different purebreds.

Designer dogs are not a breed, but a cross between two different purebred breeds. A recent study by the Institute of Canine Biology showed that cross breeds have fewer risks of inheriting genetic disorders than their purebred parents.

At the moment, breeders in the United States are selectively crossbreeding Shorkies with the hope of the class becoming a new American Kennel Club registered breed.

Photo Courtesy of Anne Kearns Fers

History of the Shorkie

The origins of the Shorkie are quite difficult to establish, but it is believed breeders in the United States first crossed the Yorkshire Terrier with a Shih Tzu to create an adorable, extremely intelligent pet that was easier to train.

One of the advantages of crossbreeding a Yorkshire Terrier and Shih Tzu is they both are around the same height. The Yorkshire Terrier is about an inch shorter than the Shih Tzu. For this reason, the Shih Tzu is the female and the Yorkie the male, since the Shih Tzu is slighter bigger, and there will be less pressure on her uterus and her body when giving birth.

Since the Shorkie's genetic information depends entirely upon the genetic data that is passed on from the parents' breeds, it's important to learn something about each parent.

Shih Tzu

The earliest recorded history of the Shih Tzu goes back to 800 B.C. in China, where it was referred to as the Lion Dog and was an integral part of the Chinese culture. The Shih Tzu was considered to be a royal escort for members of the Imperial Court. Historians believe the Shih Tzu breed found its way into Europe in the early 1900's, and in 1934, they were first registered as a breed with the Club of England.

Despite having a stubborn streak, Shih Tzu are quite easy to train due to their high level of intelligence. They are fiercely loyal to their owners, affectionate, independent, and gentle. Perhaps, this is why the Shorkie has continuously ranked number one of the Top 20 breeds, year after year, by some of the world's top kennel organizations.

However, like most purebred, Shih Tzu are not without health concerns. They are prone to suffering from hypothyroidism and intervertebral disk disease. They are also considered a brachycephalic dog breed because of their snubbed nose. This means that respiratory and dental issues are very common.

Shih Tzu are considered to be a toy breed. Their average weight can be anywhere from 9 to 15 pounds and about 9 inches tall. Even though they are prone to numerous health issues, they can live more than 15 years if they are well cared for.

Photo Courtesy of Debbie Massey

CHAPTER 1   Meet the Shorkie

Yorkshire Terrier

The Shih Tzu and the Yorkshire terrier's history could not be different. The Shih Tzu was bred specifically for royalty while the Yorkshire Terrier was bred for driving away rats that lived in Scotland in and around the wool factories.

The history of the Yorkshire terrier goes back to the early 1800's when Scottish weavers crossbred their terriers with the local dogs. Historians believe the Yorkshire terrier originally might have been a mix of a Maltese, a Paisley terrier, and a Scotch terrier. Only around the 1860's did the Yorkshire terrier begin to be bred professionally.

The Yorkshire terrier is often referred to as a 'Yorkie'. Year after year, the AKC (American Kennel Club) lists the Yorkie as one of the Top 10 dog breeds in North America.

Even though Yorkies are quite small in size, don't be fooled. They are full of self-confidence and courage. This is exemplified by their training as the world's first ever therapy dogs during World War I and World War II, comforting the wounded.

Yorkies grow to an average height of 8 to 9 inches tall from the shoulder and typically weigh around 4 to 6 pounds. Even though they are socially adaptable to young children, it isn't recommended children under the age of 8 years handle them. They require a little more time in training than the Shih Tzu, but once they are well-trained you will have one of the world's most dedicated and affectionate dogs.

Yorkies are prone to maladies, such as cataracts, bronchitis, gastro-intestinal issues, patellar luxation, Legg-Calve-Perthes syndrome and dental problems. Their silky hair is easy to care for and is considered to be hypo-allergenic.

Your Shorkie can exhibit traits from both of its parents. For this reason, I highly recommend carefully researching breeders and determining whether or not their parent dogs have any of the above health issues.

Physical Appearance and Temperament

As we mentioned above, the Shorkie can exhibit personality and physical traits from either of his parents. But there are some well-defined physical and personality traits that you can expect your Shorkie to have.

Most Shorkies will grow to an average height of eight inches tall measuring from their shoulders. Occasionally, some can grow to fourteen inches tall. Their average weight is from six to eight pounds, if they are well-cared

Photo Courtesy of Amy Collett

for, they can live from thirteen to sixteen years of age. The Shorkie is considered to be a toy-size dog.

To keep your little pup healthy, he will need to go for regular, outside walks on an average of about thirty minutes each day or a maximum of four miles a week. Since he is a toy-sized breed, his tiny body and legs can't support long walks or vigorous hikes. However, you can burn off excess energy each day by letting him run around the house and play for about thirty minutes a day. Plus, he will love spending time with you by cuddling on your lap or by your side.

The Shorkie's fur can be a wide variety of colors. Some puppies in a litter might be a solid color, or some might have a mix of colors such as black, bluish black, white, red or brown. If you prefer your puppy have a certain color of fur, consult with the breeder. A Shorkie's coat is not prone to tangles, but to maintain coat health, it is recommended to brush your pup daily.

As for their temperament, the Shorkie's parents are both renowned for being extremely affectionate, gentle, loyal and loving. So, it is to be expected your Shorkie will display similar personality traits.

They have a stubborn steak which will make them a little more challenging to train, but with persistence, schooling will pay off. Most Shorkie owners state that the hardest challenge in training their Shorkie is teaching him when not to bark. This will be discussed later in the book.

Toy-size breeds like Shorkies are often prone to suffering from hypoglycemia or a collapsed trachea. As they age, they might suffer from progressive retinal atrophy and some allergies.

Again, these are general observations about the typical characteristics of a Shorkie; these traits can and do vary.

CHAPTER 1 Meet the Shorkie

Is a Shorkie the Right Fit for You?

Shorkies are an excellent pet for experienced and first-time pet owners, as they are easy to train. But, as with most pets, they are best suited for families with certain characteristics.

Here are some general questions to ask yourself to see if you will make a good match for a Shorkie:

- Can I give him at least thirty minutes or more of quality time - playing, socializing and exercising?
- Would I be able to spend less than five minutes a day brushing his coat and other grooming necessities, such as cleaning his teeth?
- Do I have time to take him for one or two short walks daily?
- Am I disciplined enough to train him to be obedient?
- Is there someone in the house most of the day to avoid him being left alone for extended periods?
- Can I reciprocate his unfailing love he will show to me day after day?

If you decide that a Shorkie is the ideal choice for you and your family, you are not just getting a pet, you are gaining a new member of the family that will be dedicated to showing his new loved-ones how much he adores them.

Photo Courtesy of Sarah Betros

CHAPTER 2
Choosing a Shorkie

Your new Shorkie is going to be part of your life for the next ten years or more. Instead of picking up the first adorable puppy you see, you will need to research the breeder and make a background check into the health of your Shorkie's parents, etc. Dogs are for life, so you want to make sure you are getting a healthy puppy.

In this chapter, we will discuss the pros and cons of getting a puppy vs. an older dog who is up for adoption. Also, we will learn how to find a reputable breeder and what questions you should ask them before signing the contract. Above all, we will consider everything you need to know about how to pick the ideal puppy for your lifestyle. The decision to get a Shorkie should not be an impulsive one.

Photo Courtesy of Charris Quijano

CHAPTER 2   Choosing a Shorkie

Buying vs. Adopting

Should you buy your Shorkie or adopt from your local shelter?

There really is no simple way to answer that question as it basically depends on your personal criteria when it comes to your new future companion. To help you answer this controversial question, here are some of the pros and cons of each option to take into consideration.

One of the main reasons that pet owners decide to buy a Shorkie is because they will be able to train him from an early age, which means there will be no bad habits that might be hard to break. Often new pet owners will bring home their new companion between the age of eight weeks to twelve weeks, which gives them the opportunity to form a special bond with the puppy that will last a lifetime.

Most pet owners decide to buy their puppy because they want to make sure it is healthy and want to be familiar with their dog's lineage and family health history. Another advantage is they can see the breeder's past health and pedigree certificates for the parent dogs.

Other pet owners choose to buy their Shorkie because the cost of adopting sometimes is more expensive than purchasing a puppy. Plus, many rescue organizations have a strict screening process, and not everyone who applies is accepted.

Still other pet owners shy away from purchasing a puppy because they prefer to adopt an older dog that is already house-trained, vaccinated and spayed. Perhaps, they don't have the time or energy to train a young dog, or they feel they lack experience in obedience training.

Other pet owners feel quite strongly against buying from a breeder. The sad reality is every year in the United States more than one million cats and dogs are euthanized because of a lack of space in shelters. Because of this, many new pet owners open their hearts to give a home to a dog in need – one who comes from a shelter.

Finding a rescue Shorkie at your local shelter might be harder than buying from a breeder because they are a new designer breed. Thus, there might not be too many options. However, if your heart is set on adopting

> **HELPFUL TIP**
> **Hypoallergenic**
>
> Shorkies are a popular choice for allergy sufferers because of their hypoallergenic coat. Their fur is medium-long and more like human hair than other non-hypoallergenic breeds. While there is no such thing as a 100% hypoallergenic dog, allergies are caused by pet dander which is attached to your pet's fur. So, a low-shedding dog such as a Shorkie will produce less dander.

Photo Courtesy of Meaghan Flynn

a Shorkie, then I recommend checking social media and the Internet for different rescue organizations. Before committing to adopt from any type of rescue organization, do some online research to make sure the organizations are reputable and trustworthy.

If you decide that you want to adopt a Shorkie, you will want to make sure he is a good candidate for you and your family. When you go to the shelter, observe the dog you want to adopt and how he interacts with you. Does he come to the front of his cage, or does he huddle in the back? Does his tail wag when you talk to him in a gentle voice? When you pet him, does he relax or become agitated?

Whether you decide to buy or adopt, do not be shy about asking questions, either to the breeder or the shelter. A reputable breeder or shelter will be very direct and transparent about their practices, and they will try to answer any question you have in order to help you make the best decision, not only for you but for your future dog.

CHAPTER 2   Choosing a Shorkie

Shelters and Rescues

Bringing a rescue dog home is a win-win for both of you. Unfortunately, there is a stigma surrounding shelter dogs, often assuming they have behavioral issues and are unpredictable.

However, this belief could not be further from the truth. The majority of dogs in shelters are there not because of the dog's behavior but simply because their previous family had a change in circumstances. Most are just unlucky dogs waiting for a loving home.

Advantages of adopting:
- By adopting a Shorkie, you save his life and create space in the shelter for another dog in need.
- Shelter dogs save you money in vet fees as most shelter dogs are already spayed or neutered and microchipped.
- Often shelter dogs are already potty-trained, which will save you time and energy.
- There are no unexpected surprises when it comes to the dog's personality as the shelter will inform you beforehand about your dog.
- Shelter dogs are extremely loving and grateful to their new owners for rescuing them.
- Adopting from a shelter is considerably more affordable when compared to buying from a professional breeder.
- You are supporting a nonprofit organization dedicated to caring for neglected cats and dogs.

Disadvantages of adopting:
- You will miss out on the puppy stage of your dog's life as most rescue dogs are eight months and older
- Sometimes the shelter might not have an accurate background of your dog's family history
- Depending on the shelter, there might be a long list of requirements to qualify for adopting a dog

According to the Animal Humane Society, adoption fees for dogs and puppies can run from $120 to $670, depending on the shelter. On the other hand, buying a Shorkie from a reputable breeder can cost anywhere from $700 upwards to $2000. You can expect to pay even more if you buy a puppy with breeding rights.

Shorkies are a relatively new designer breed, so it might take a little more time to find one that is available for adoption, but it is not impossible.

Photo Courtesy of Lisa Whymark

CHAPTER 2   Choosing a Shorkie

Shelters and rescues know their dogs and want them to go to good homes. Ask them if you can be informed when a Shorkie shows up. Another option is to seek out local rescues that specialize in relocating Shorkies to new homes.

What are the requirements to adopt a dog from a shelter or rescue? Each shelter or rescue has different requirements before starting the adoption process.

The following is a general guideline - the requirements might vary from each intuition:

- Most shelters will require you to show a government-issued photo ID proving you are twenty-one years or older.
- You will need to fill out an application form that might be straight-forward, or it might be an in-depth questionnaire.
- In some cases, you will need to provide references, such as permission from your landlord verifying you are allowed to have pets.
- Home visit - some shelters or rescues will send a representative to make sure your home is safe and suitable for a dog.
- Meet and greet - the shelter will observe how you and your family interact with the dog before taking him home.
- Adoption fee and costs will vary depending on the institution. Generally, the fee covers basic veterinary care, food, housing and care the dog received while in the rescue.

As mentioned above, this is a just a general guideline for adoption requirements. Shelters and rescues have the sole motive to find a loving home for the dog and to prevent him from ending up again in the same situation in the future.

How to Find a Reputable Breeder

When we mention a reputable breeder, we are NOT referring to a puppy mill. Puppy mills are inhumane and unethical. They keep the puppy's parents in deplorable conditions, and the parent dogs are only used for one purpose - breeding. Often once they are unable to reproduce, they are put to sleep. On the other hand, a reputable breeder will treat their dogs as part of the family, caring for all of their emotional and physical needs.

One of the best ways to find a reputable breeder is by word of mouth, perhaps a relative or a friend purchased a Shorkie from them in the past. Ask them about their experience with the breeder, etc. Inquire about a reputable breeder they would recommend.

I also highly recommend asking local veterinarians about reputable breeders.

Once you have narrowed down your list to two or three breeders that seem to fit your criteria, ask if you can meet the future puppy's parents in person. In the event they refuse to allow you to come to their house or if they suggest meeting in another location, then a red flag should go up. If they do not want you to visit the facility, then it probably is a puppy mill.

When you go to the breeder's facility, you will be able to observe how the breeders care for their dogs. The dogs and puppies should have a clean-living environment with fresh water, a designated area for the bathroom and sleeping. Also, look around for any play toys laying around to keep their dogs entertained. Look at the dogs for any signs of malnutrition, such as protruding ribs or any signs of illness such as runny noses, sores, rough patches of fur, etc. All of this will give you a good indication about whether or not you can trust the breeder.

A sound breeder normally will want to build a good rapport with you, so they should quickly and openly answer any of your questions. If they are wishy-washy or vague about something, there is another red flag!

Another warning signal that they should not be trusted is if they ask you to pick up your puppy before it is eight weeks old. Puppies need at least eight to twelve weeks to learn proper socialization skills from their mother and their littermates.

The average cost for a Shorkie could be anywhere between $600 to $2000, depending on his parent's lineage. A cheaper price tag, can be a clear indicator that he was bred by a puppy mill.

Important Questions to Ask the Breeder

You can never ask a breeder too many questions.

Most reputable breeders will also want to interview you before they agree to sell you one of their puppies as they care about the future of their dogs. Often, they will ask questions related to your family, your lifestyle, and if you have other pets, etc. This will give them a glimpse into the type of living conditions you plan to provide for your Shorkie.

You should request to see any paperwork related to your Shorkie's parents' health and if possible, the family, to make sure there is not a history of interbreeding. Also, if your Shorkies parents are purebreds, there should be a history about their general health or genetic defects going back at least three generations.

You can also ask for any references from fellow breeders, veterinarians, past clients, etc. This will give you a better idea of whether or not you are

Photo Courtesy of Sydney Cervantes

dealing with a trustworthy breeder. Some other questions you might want to ask: How long have they been breeding Shorkies? How many times a year do they have a litter? Have the parents been registered with the Orthopedic Foundation for Animals?

Finding the right breeder is just as important as picking out the best puppy of the litter for you and your family.

Breeder Contracts and Guarantees

Often, we think of contracts and guarantees when we buy a car, but we never really associate those words with buying a dog. However, most reputable breeders have contracts and guarantees as a protection for themselves and for you, the buyer.

Most breeders will make you sign a contract and request a down payment toward the purchase of the puppy even before your Shorkie is born. If you back out of the contract without a valid reason before it is time to pick up the puppy, you will most likely lose your down payment.

The purpose of most breeder contracts is to share their advice, expectations and ideology concerning the dog they are handing over to you. By signing your name on the contract, it is a solemn reminder of the huge undertaking of which you have agreed to be responsible.

Many breeders include a clause in the contract that, if you become unable to care for your dog, they have the right to take your puppy from you. This avoids owners dumping their dogs in shelters or even on the street. Furthermore, the contract gives breeders legal power to rescue the dog from bad living conditions.

Most breeders will want you to sign a clause stating you will get your puppy spayed or neutered by a certain age and you will not use the puppy for any type of breeding. If you plan on using your Shorkie for breeding, he will cost more, and the contract will be more explicit about future health screenings, etc.

If there is anything in the contract you have difficulty understanding or are unsure about, do not sign the contract. Make sure you understand completely what you are signing beforehand. You can ask the breeder to send you a copy of contract, so you can read it carefully without feeling pressured.

Even though your breeder has done everything in their power to ensure you are getting a healthy puppy, health issues can arise unexpectedly. Good breeders will include in their health guarantee a section against genetic defects, normally up to a certain age. Often a good breeder will be willing to refund the money or replace your puppy if he suffers from a genetically linked illness in his lifetime. To avoid this, it is highly recommended to see the health history of your Shorkies' parents.

Male vs. Female

Now that you have decided on the breeder and all the other details, the breeder will probably ask you whether you prefer a male or a female.

Most veterinarians and professional dog trainers will tell you that your dog's sex will have little bearing on the dog's personality and their ability to adapt to your lifestyle. Whether your dog is a male or a female, its personality will be most influenced by surroundings and training. However, there are some anatomical, hormonal, health and behavior differences of which you should be aware.

Anatomical differences: Male dogs tend to be larger than female dogs when they are fully grown. However, female dog will reach maturity faster than a male dog, often resulting in an easier dog to train.

Hormonal differences: An unneutered male dog will have the urge to mark his territory every few feet by peeing on something. Also, they have the tendency to mount other dogs, and they may try to escape to pursue female dogs. An unspayed female dog will experience a heat cycle twice a year. By spaying and neutering your dog before it reaches the age of maturity, you will almost completely eliminate these mating behaviors.

Health differences: Studies have shown that an unspayed female dog can develop mammary cancer or uterine infections later in life. Unneutered male dogs have a greater risk of developing testicular cancer or benign prostatic hyperplasia. Most vets will recommend spaying or neutering your dog as it improves their overall health and helps prevent orthopedic issues as they age.

Behavior differences: Your dog's personality will be directly influenced by training and upbringing. Studies have shown dogs get along better with the opposite sex when they have received proper training by their owner. So, if you are planning to bring another puppy into the family, you might consider getting a different sex than the puppy you currently own.

In the end, instead of concentrating on the sex of your dog, make sure the dog or the puppy's personality and temperament is a good fit for your family and your lifestyle.

Picking the Correct Puppy for You

Seeing your future puppy interact with his littermates and his mother can give you an idea of his temperament and his personality.

Puppies born into a family-home environment will be more socially adjusted and accustomed to the hustle and bustle of a normal household. A puppy should be confident around strangers and should approach you

CHAPTER 2   Choosing a Shorkie

without looking anxious. If he seems wary around you or the breeder, then he may grow up to be a nervous dog.

Often, new pet owners choose the boldest puppy – the one that pushes his way to the front, but he may grow up to be a pushy, aggressive dog that is harder to train. Take the time to befriend a quieter puppy that already has good manners. However, be wary of the puppy that tucks his tail between his legs or pulls away when you try to scratch behind his ears. A shy puppy could grow into an adult dog that is easily startled or frightened and could snap at you or your children.

> **HELPFUL TIP**
> **Is Adoption an Option?**
>
> Since Shorkies are a relatively new breed, you're unlikely to be able to find an adoption organization that is solely dedicated to Shorkies. If adoption is important to you, get in contact with your local Humane Society and other canine rescues in your area to find the perfect fit. When adopting, always get as much background information as you can to ease your pet's transition to its new home.

Make sure your Shorkie is in good health by choosing a puppy that has clean ears with no strange odors. Also, his eyes should be bright and alert to his surroundings. Take a peek in his mouth to check out the health of his teeth and his gums. He should have soft, shiny fur that doesn't look greasy or tattered. Plus, there should be no sign of fleas or ring worm.

Take your time to evaluate each of the puppies, and watch how he interacts when he is apart from or with his littermates. His reactions and behavior can be an indication as to how he will act in your house.

If the litter of puppies does not look healthy, etc., no matter how adorable they are and how much your heart breaks for them, walk away. Sometimes, walking away without a puppy is the best choice because it will save lots of heart break in the future.

CHAPTER 3
What to Expect for the First Few Months

Bringing a new dog into your life is not without some challenges the first few months, but the joys will outweigh any of the inconveniences you might experience. Thankfully, a puppy's general behavior and development is pretty straight forward and predictable. Preparing for your new Shorkie can make the transition smoother for the entire family and for your new dog.

Photo Courtesy of Emily Ree

CHAPTER 3   What to Expect for the First Few Months

Puppy-Proofing Your Home – Inside and Out

Before you bring your new dog home, you will need to puppy-proof your home. Creating a safe environment inside and outside of your home involves removing any and all dangers. Your Shorkie will be extremely curious and will explore every nook and cranny of your house. All of that exploring can get him into some serious trouble!

Puppies will chew on anything they can fit into their mouth, plus their body coordination is not very graceful, so they will bump into things or break fragile items with their tail. Plus, they cannot tell the difference between their chew toys and your favorite leather shoes! It is up to you to protect your Shorkie and to keep your stuff safe.

> **HELPFUL TIP**
> **Choosing the Right Bed**
>
> Shorkies are relatively small dogs and require smaller beds than their larger counterparts. But choosing the perfect bed may take some time. Depending on how your dog likes to sleep, you may find that he prefers one style of bed over another. For example, if your Shorkie enjoys sleeping spread out on his stomach or back, you may need a longer bed without high sides. But if your dog enjoys curling up in a quiet corner of the house, an enclosed bed might be the right option.

As you go through each room, get down to your puppy's level to inspect the area where your four-pawed friend will be spending the majority of his time. By doing this, you will be able to easily identify any potential dangers your Shorkie could chew on or get all tangled up in.

Another fundamental detail is the entire family needs to know and understand what represents a danger for your new puppy. Get the family involved in puppy-proofing your home. This will help them be more proactive in their pick-up routine. Creating a safe environment isn't enough, maintaining it day after day is the key.

A few days before your puppy comes home, take your time and walk through each room of your house – one last time to remove any of these potential hazards:

In the kitchen – The kitchen is a fascinating place for any dog as there are all sorts of interesting smells and odors. All of those nooks and crannies to crawl into and explore are a pure temptation for a curious puppy. Invest in childproof latches for your cupboards to prevent your puppy from accessing potentially harmful foods or even your cleaning supplies under the sink.

Block off access to any open bags of food, etc. in your kitchen or your pantry. Dogs digest food differently than humans, and many human foods can lead to serious health problems for a dog or even death. You can find an extensive list of foods that are toxic for dogs in Chapter Ten of this book.

Your Shorkie is half Yorkshire terrier, so he has inherited an excellent sniffing nose and can smell stinky garbage more than a mile away! Place your garbage in a tightly enclosed container, preferably placed under the sink.

A wet tile floor is a huge hazard for your dog as he can accidently slide into something and seriously hurt himself. Another hazard can be a loose throw rug on a tile or wooden floor. Your puppy could easily trip, or even worse, the rug could slip while he is playing causing him to crash into something.

In the living or family room – Your living areas have all sorts of items to tempt your teething Shorkie. You would be surprised how much food is under your table or couch. Your dog will sniff it out and gobble it up faster than you can snap your fingers! Your Shorkie will try to chew on any visible electrical cords while teething, so block off the cords with heavy furniture or place them inside a PVC cord protector.

Your living area is where you and your family spend most of your time, so it can quickly become a disorganized space. Be vigilant to keep everything in its place and off the floor. Keep magazines, iPads, shoes, pillows, blankets, etc. away from your Shorkie's reach.

Another hazard that is commonly overlooked are the cords for your curtains or blinds. Your curious puppy could easily become tangled up in them,

Photo Courtesy of Carrie Moore

causing him to have a deadly accident. Your Shorkie will use his tongue to explore your house, including your electrical outlets. Be sure to cover any unused outlets with a childproof cap.

In the bedroom – Shorkies have a high sense of smell and will be attracted to anything that smells like you, such as your clothing, shoes and slippers. If these items are not behind closed doors, your puppy will use them as one of his new chewing toys.

Place dirty clothes into a closed laundry hamper, pick up any clothes and towels from the floor and put them where they belong. Put any smaller ingestible items, such as hair ties, loose change, jewelry, etc., in a secure container or drawer. Secure any electrical cords or television wires. If you do not want you dog going under your bed, be sure to block access with boxes.

In the office – Your office is like a candy store to a kid. Your puppy will have so many chewable temptations, such as pens and pencils, cords and wires, paperclips, rubber bands, magazines and staples, etc. Even though these items might seem harmless to the average eye, if ingested they can be fatal. Just as with the rest of the house, pick up any small items and secure electrical cords or wires.

House plants hold another threat for your Shorkie, as many are toxic for dogs if ingested. Place them on a shelf or countertop, so they're out of your dog's reach. If they are too big to place on a shelf, perhaps place them in a room where your puppy can't access, at least until he has outgrown his teething phase.

In the bathroom – The bathroom can be a hazardous place your Shorkie with medicine, soap, razors, cotton balls and cleaning supplies, and these items can be easily ingested if left within his reach. Make sure each member of your family is aware of the dangers, and they clean up after themselves. Place any soaps, shampoos, accessories and cleaning supplies inside a cabinet or on a shelf.

When your dog is still a curious puppy, it is especially important to keep the toilet bowl lid closed at all times. It would only take a mischievous puppy seconds to jump into the toilet bowl and drown. Do not forget to make sure the trash bin has a locking lid or stash it inside a cabinet. Secure the drawers and cabinets with childproof latches and tuck those dangling cords out of your puppies reach.

If you have medications or vitamin supplements on a shelf for easy access or a daily reminder, make sure they are tightly closed. If they would accidently spill to the ground, they can be easily ingested by your dog, meaning an emergency visit to the vet.

In the garage and yard – Even though your Shorkie will be spending the majority of his time inside of the house, you will still need to puppy-proof your garage and yard. Your garage is full of dangers for your dog, such as paint thinner, rat poison, antifreeze, fertilizers and so much more. All dogs are attracted to the sweet smell of antifreeze, but just a few drops can be fatal. Secure all dangerous items on a shelf, inside of a closed cabinet or a large cardboard box.

Walk through your yard in your bare feet, looking for any small prodding items that could easily be ingested by your dog. If you have a fence, make sure there are no openings he could squeeze under. Some flowers are toxic to dogs if consumed, such as daffodils, foxglove and lupine. If you have such flowers, be sure to block access to them while your dog is outside.

Access to stairs – Shorkies are a toy-sized dog breed, so even falling down a few stairs for them could cause broken bones. If you have stairs in your house, please purchase a pet gate to block all access in order to avoid serious injury to your Shorkie. All family members need to make a conscientious effort about keeping the pet gate properly closed at all times.

Photo Courtesy of Crystal Harshman

CHAPTER 3 What to Expect for the First Few Months

Shopping List

Once you bring home your new dog, you will not have time or will not want to leave your adorable, four-pawed best friend alone to go shopping. Before you pick up your puppy, you will want to make sure to get the following items to make him feel at home and comfortable. Of course, the following list is only a suggestion and you might discover you need more items later on.

Puppy toys – Shorkies love playing and chewing on squeaky toys, which will be your best friend when he is teething. If you are unsure what type of toys to buy for your new dog, ask your local pet shop or look online for packages of play toys for small-sized dogs. I like to take a small, plush toy with me when I pick up a new puppy and rub it on his littermates and mom, so I can bring home a comforting smell for my new puppy.

Crate – If you are planning on crate training your Shorkie, then you are going to need a crate. Look for a crate that is designed for your dog when he is full-sized. He should have enough room to stand up, stretch and completely turn around. We will discuss at full length everything you need to know about crate training in chapter Five of this book.

There are two types of crates – plastic and wire. Plastic crates are more practical for traveling.

However, I personally prefer metal crates for the following reasons:
- Wire crates can easily be collapsed and can take up less space in storage. Plastic crates only come in two pieces, and they take up more space.
- Some puppies can feel claustrophobic in a plastic pen, as there is less visibility. Wire crates provide more visibility, allowing your pup to see everything around him. When he needs quiet time, I can easily place a blanket on top.
- The majority of wire crates come with a divider that allows you to adjust the size of the crate as your puppy grows.
- The plastic tray on the bottom of the crate makes for easy clean up as it simply slides up and makes cleaning up an accident quite easy. Plastic crates will need to disabled to thoroughly disinfect.

Food and water dishes – Avoid purchasing cheap, plastic food dishes as they often contain dyes that can seep into your dog's water and food, causing allergies or skin and eye irritation. Instead, buy him stainless steel water and food dishes that can be washed in the dish washer.

Puppy bed – Even though you will probably be crate training your Shorkie, he will still need a puppy bed for the crate and another one for him

Photo Courtesy of Amanda Quach

to use while relaxing with you either on the sofa or on the floor. Look for a puppy bed that has a removable cover for easy washing and is big enough for him to grow into it. Trust me, he will love a clean, comfy bed!

Training leash and collar – A collar should have a space for your dog's personal information, and a training leash often comes with a no-pull harness, which will protect your tiny pups' trachea. Plus, it will teach him not to pull while out on walks around the block. Trust me – again, he will love the harness.

Toothpaste and toothbrush – You should try to get your puppy used to having his teeth brushed starting from the first week of bringing him home. Never ever use a human tooth paste on your dog because most human toothpaste contains an artificial sweetener called Xylitol, which is extremely toxic to dogs. Instead, buy a toothpaste specifically designed for dogs and a toothbrush made for small-sized dogs.

Training pads – Since your Shorkie will be spending the majority of his time inside the house, you will need to house-train him. One of the most efficient ways to potty-train your puppy is by using pee pads, as they are easy to clean up and to move around. Often smaller dogs are weary of conventional litter boxes as they are harder to get into.

Stain and odor remover – No matter how strict you are when it comes to house training, your little guy is going to have an accident or two. Look for an odor remover that destroys enzymes that are often left behind in the urine. These enzymes are like a beacon on a lighthouse, calling for your dog to return to that same spot to urinate there. So, make sure you have a cleaner that is powerful enough.

Doggy treats – You must start training your dog to understand good behavior from day one... and treats are essential! There is a wide assortment of doggy treats available on the market.

Nail trimmer – Look for a pair of nail trimmers that is designed for the toy-size breeds. It should be a good quality as it needs to last a long time. Check out the reviews online to make sure the trimmers are easy to use.

Puppy brush – Shorkies have fine fur and will need to be brushed daily to prevent his coat from becoming tangled or matted. The first few brushings, try to get him used to the brush by letting him smell it first and then gently brushing him for less than a minute at a time and rewarding him with a treat at the end.

Puppy gate and play pen – A puppy gate can block access to areas where you do not want your Shorkie to go, such as the stairs or outside. A play pen will also prevent your dog from getting into trouble when you are unable to keep a close eye on him and when you do not necessarily want to lock him up in his crate.

Establish Puppy House Rules and Daily Routines

Establishing house rules and a daily routine for the new dog are essential, especially if there is more than one person living in your house. This is important to help maintain consistency. Your Shorkie will be eager to adapt

Photo Courtesy of Jessica Price

CHAPTER 3   What to Expect for the First Few Months

to his new family and understand what is expected of him. The more consistent the entire household is in following these regulations, the easier and faster he will figure everything out.

Before you bring your Shorkie home, sit down with your family to discuss and agree on the following points:

Where will he sleep? For a small dog like a Shorkie, I recommend placing the crate in someone's bedroom for at least a year or until he is housetrained.

Is he allowed on the furniture? Shorkies are lap dogs, so they will love sitting next to you or on your lap. Will he be allowed on all the furniture or just the couch but not the bed?

Who will feed him? Your Shorkie will need to eat two or three times a day at a specific time, depending on the instructions from your breeder. If your child will feed the dog, teach them to place the food in a clean dish and then move away to allow him to eat peacefully.

Where will he be during the day? If someone in your household works from home, then the best place would be by their side in a play pen with their crate. For the first few weeks, he will need regular bathroom breaks approximately every hour or two. Plan on someone being home each day to puppy-sit.

How will you train him? I highly recommend you train your Shorkie by using positive reinforcement training methods. For more information about this, please see chapter seven of this book. Choose one primary trainer and have the whole family help in reinforcing the new behavior.

I know bringing home a new dog can be very exciting. For your puppy, it can seem overwhelming and exhausting. Phone ahead of time to tell your friends and families you will not be having guests over to meet him for the first day.

If you have children, teach them how to pick up the puppy or pet him by using a stuffed toy. Even though they will want to play with the new dog constantly, they need to give him his space to explore his new home and to rest. Young children tend to yell or shout, so warn your children to use their indoor voices around the new dog to avoid startling him.

If you already have a resident pet, make sure you have created a new puppy sanctuary. Your pre-existing pet should still be able to access areas where he previously was allowed; otherwise, he will think he is being punished. If possible, ask the breeder beforehand to give you a piece of cloth that has the new puppy's scent. Introduce the scent to your current pet. By doing this, you will help your pet quickly embrace the new dog into your home.

The Ride Home

Finally, the day has arrived to pick up your new best friend! Make sure you are prepared by bringing along a blanket or towel, something to chew on, the leash and collar plus any cleaning supplies you might need if there is an accident in the car.

The breeder should give you a small bag of the food your puppy is currently eating to help you wean him onto the new food that you plan to feed him. No food should be given to the dog two to three hours prior to traveling; if the trip is longer than three hours, be sure to bring a few pieces of food in case he gets hungry.

Before you start driving home, take your new best friend for a short walk so he can get used to being near to you. Another plus is that he probably will go to the bathroom outside before getting into the car.

But how should you transport your new dog home? Should he be placed inside a cardboard box on the floor or in a traveling crate? Or should he sit on your lap and be allowed to roam about the car freely? Is it better for him to sit in the back-seat versus the front seat? Here are some common concerns:

Safety – Puppies are curious by nature and if they are not secured inside their crate, they will quickly start exploring their new surroundings inside of the car. He could easily squeeze under the back seat and end up under the driver's feet. Another risk is he could accidently fall off the seat if the car suddenly has to swerve around a corner or come to a quick stop.

Front or back seat – Young children are not permitted to sit in the front seat due to the hazard of the air bags. In the case of an accident and the air bag is activated, the airbag's force can seriously harm or result in death of a young child. There would be an even greater risk of injury for a small dog such as a Shorkie.

To crate or to carry? – The crate will prevent your new best friend taking any unwanted excursions on the drive home. In addition, it will prevent him from getting hurt or having an accident in your car. Before you place the crate in the back seat of the car, place it outside and put a treat inside. Let your Shorkie investigate and go into the crate on his own terms. The dog must feel safe and sound inside of his crate. Place a familiar toy or blanket inside of the crate.

Travel carriers or crates are the safest way to transport your dog inside of your car; plus, the crate can be used to take your dog to the vet or on exciting adventures in the future

The following points you should consider:

- **Find the correct size** - A twelve-week old Shorkie weighs approximately five ounces and should be the size of large tea cup. A fully grown Shorkie

CHAPTER 3 What to Expect for the First Few Months

will weigh between twelve to fourteen pounds and range from six to fourteen inches in height. The carrier or crate should be big enough for your pup to stand up in and to turn around.

- **Design matters** – Car travel has many safety concerns. Look for a dog carrier that has passed third-party crash tests and comes highly reviewed. A poorly designed dog carrier can be even more hazardous in an accident.
- **Choose a style** – There are two basic styles of travel carriers for dogs – hard and soft cover. Hard covers offer superior protection for your

Photo Courtesy of Sandra Cadieux

dog and are preferable if traveling long distances. Soft covers offer less protection for your dog but are easier to carry than the heavy, cumbersome hard cover carriers.

Psychological well-being – One of the biggest concerns on the drive home is your Shorkie's psychological well-being. You will be separating him from his family, where he felt safe and protected. You need to make the whole experience a positive one, so you do not create emotional scars that could resurface later on in his life, such as separation anxiety.

Talk to him warmly inside the car and gently caress him making him feel safe and secure. Ask a friend or family member to drive the car, so you can sit in the back seat next to the crate on the trip home. If you play music inside of the car, select tones that are more subdued and transmit tranquility.

Climatic control inside of the car – Puppies, in general, have a difficult time thermoregulating their body's temperature. Hence, they have a greater risk of hypothermia and hyperthermia. Make sure the inside temperature of the car is comfortable. If for any reason, you need to get out of the car, do not leave him alone in the vehicle.

Bathroom breaks – On the road home, if you have to make a bathroom stop for your puppy, choose a spot that is not visited by too many other dogs. Your puppy probably has not been vaccinated yet, and you do not want him getting sick.

The First Day

Bringing home your new Shorkie is a very exciting and happy occasion. Even though you and your family have been counting the days until your new pup comes home, for your puppy, everything is new for him, and it can be a terrifying experience.

Remember your new Shorkie is still a tiny baby, who has spent his whole life staying close to his mom and his littermates. Everything he ever knew is gone - the smells, noises and sights have all changed. It is of utmost importance you reassure him he is safe by making him feel at home as soon as possible. Often the breeder will send a puppy home with a piece of his blanket, etc., so he will have a familiar smell from his old home.

Let your new Shorkie dictate how he wants to interact with his new surroundings. Some dogs will immediately start exploring and climbing all over their new family. Others will be a little more standoffish and take a little more time to embrace his new family. Feel free to pet him softly and talk to him but let him come to you. By doing this, you will teach your puppy they can trust you, your family and his new surroundings.

CHAPTER 3 What to Expect for the First Few Months

Be patient with your new Shorkie as he tries to adapt and settle into his new life. Let him move freely around the house, exploring each room. Show him his bathroom area and his water and food dishes.

Avoid loud noises and jerky movements. If you have small children in the house, carefully supervise them as they interact with the new puppy. Discourage any friends or family from coming over the first day to meet the new puppy as meeting even more new people can be overwhelming for the new dog. The first day is about bonding with his new family.

If you normally work on the day you plan to bring your Shorkie home, make sure you request time off, so you can spend as much time with the puppy as possible. After all, it is the first day that you embark on an incredibly, special friendship!

Photo Courtesy of Sarah Betros

First Night

It is nighttime and you are probably exhausted. It has been an emotional day not only for you but for your new Shorkie. Puppies normally sleep fifteen to twenty hours each day, but they need to go to the bathroom every one to two hours. Whenever they wake up, they are need to go to the bathroom... fast. So, have a spot close by and run!

I have to warn you the first few nights you will be sleep deprived until your new Shorkie adapts to your schedule. He will probably wake you up a few times each night by barking or crying. So, place the crate in the area where you want him to sleep. Some people want their puppy to sleep in their bedroom, others in the living room, etc.

Be sure to place a mama-scented blanket, towel or soft-stuffed toy inside the crate with him. Your little Shorkie has a strong sense of smell, and he is most likely overwhelmed by all the new scents. Having something from his old home will help him feel more safe and secure.

Another trick to remind him of his mother and littermates is to put an old-fashioned alarm clock under his blanket. The tick-tock of the alarm clock mimics the heartbeat of his mom and littermates. Another idea to make a puppy feel more at home is by placing a hot water bottle under his blanket at night.

From the very first night, you need to start teaching your Shorkie bedtime is sleepy time and not playtime. If he barks to go the bathroom, take him to the designated bathroom area. Once he goes to the bathroom, reward him with a treat, and then take him back to his crate to go back to sleep. Do not be fooled by those big brown eyes! He needs to learn nighttime is for sleeping, not for playing.

Your new pup's bladder has not built up enough control to get through the entire night without needing to go to the bathroom. It will take a number of weeks before you will be able to sleep through the night without having to rush him to his bathroom spot. Expect to get up at least five to six times the first few nights to take him to the bathroom.

First Vet Visit

Many veterinarians suggest you bring a dog in for a meet-and-greet before the actual visit for his vaccinations. This will help the dog associate the vet's office with a positive experience, especially since the employees will probably slip him a treat or two.

Reputable veterinarians are busy and do not have time for drop-ins unless it is an emergency. Therefore, make an appointment for your

Shorkie's first visit and try to arrive a few minutes early, so he can get used to his surroundings, noises and smells.

When you go in for the first visit, be sure to take with you any paperwork relating to your dog, such as vaccination and health records from the breeder or shelter. Most likely this paperwork will stay in your Shorkie's personal file at the veterinarian's office.

What to expect during the first visit? The veterinarian will weigh your puppy, check his temperature through the rectum, examine his eyes, ears, mouth, teeth, feet, genital region and fur. He will listen to his heartbeat and lungs by using a stethoscope and palpate his lymph nodes and abdomen area. Then he will administer any required vaccines, de-wormers, etc.

The vet will also discuss future medical procedures he might need, such as spaying or neutering and microchipping. Remember, to follow the vaccination schedule and follow-up on any future required visits.

Obedience Classes

Obedience training has never been easier! You can find hundreds of trustworthy and highly recommended professional dog obedience classes online.

Whether you have a three-month-old puppy or an older dog, obedience classes are very beneficial to help your new dog learn to respect you and to teach him how to fit in with his new family. Puppy obedience classes are structured for puppies under the age of six months and teach basic commands, socializing with other dogs and how to greet people without jumping up on them. Most obedience courses will focus on using a clicker and giving rewards for positive behavior.

Obedience classes for more mature dogs will focus on learning good manners and on reinforcing basic commands, but they will also introduce new commands, such as stay, lie down, roll over and how to heel while on the leash. In Chapter Eight, we will discuss everything you need to know about how to successfully train your dog.

Teach your dog what you expect of him and you will see how hard he tries to please you. The best part is the end result will be that you have a well-trained dog and a closer relationship because you will mutually understand each other.

CHAPTER 4
Laying a Solid Foundation to Train Your Shorkie

A dog's bad behavior is a direct result of bad parenting and bad training. It is not the dog's fault.

Bad behavior leads to strained relationships between both the pet owner and the dog. Most dogs are willing to learn, but they just need to be taught how to accomplish that learning. In this chapter, we will discuss how you can avoid some common training mistakes and how to nip bad behavior in the bud.

Photo Courtesy of Solange Moreno

CHAPTER 4 Laying a Solid Foundation to Train Your Shorkie

Photo Courtesy of Nicole Petrone

Disobedient or Bad Parenting?

Your style of puppy parenting will have a direct impact on your dog's behavior. There really is no such thing as an untrainable dog. Their natural instinct is to adapt and to obey their owners' commands. However, on the other hand, there is such a thing as a bad puppy parent. Avoid some of these common mistakes:

You lack consistency – Training techniques need be straight forward and clear for your dog to understand. If you keep changing the technique or varying the method of training, your dog will just get confused and bored of learning. For example, your dog is allowed on the couch somedays but not others. This is confusing to the animal. If you set rules, you need to stick to them.

Photo Courtesy of Sandra McElrea

You get too emotional – Your dog is very sensitive to your emotions. If he sees that you are getting agitated, upset or even a little irritated, you will turn your training sessions into torture. Or perhaps you tend to get over-excited when your puppy finally obeys you. You start squealing and yelling out of happiness; that energy can cause your dog to become distracted and over-excited, too. Both scenarios will cause your dog to lose focus and interest in learning.

Lack of confidence – Dogs need a leader, and they can sense when their human parents lack confidence. If you show you feel insecure or unsure about how to train your dog, he will exploit your weakness to his benefit. If you feel you are unable to teach him, then take a couple of obedience classes together. This will give you confidence.

You praise bad behavior – One of the biggest mistakes I see new pet owners make over and over again is considering bad behavior to be cute. Instead of telling your puppy not to bark at the television, you praise him or maybe get out the camera to take some pictures of him. Not correcting his bad behavior when he is still a puppy will only reinforce that behavior and create a habit. Bad behavior is never acceptable - no matter how cute your puppy looks. Think of it this way. Would you think it is cute when your puppy is a grown-up dog? No, you would not.

You are not being proactive – Most new pet owners tend to overreact when their new dog makes a mistake instead of seizing the opportunity to teach them what behavior is acceptable. For example, imagine you are trying to teach your Shorkie not to bark. Instead of waiting for him to bark and telling him that he is a bad boy, try to distract him just before he is going to bark with another activity that is more acceptable. By being proactive instead of reactive, you are reprogramming his brain to eliminate bad behavior and replace it with good behavior. Try it, this method does work.

HELPFUL TIP
From Affectionate to Clingy

Shorkies in general are a loveable and affectionate breed, which leads many people to choose them for companion dogs. But too much attention can lead to your dog become clingy, or cause separation anxiety in your dog when you're not around. Crate training may help prevent property destruction when leaving your dog alone for short periods of time, but proper training from a young age is the key to preventing clinginess in your Shorkie.

How to Teach an Old Dog New Tricks

Can you teach an old dog new tricks? Yes, it just depends on the pet owner!

Older dogs might have more limitations than a younger dog, such as mobility and physical issues; however, despite these challenges, adult dogs can learn new tricks. The key is understanding the positive reinforcement method, which is a large dose of patience, reward training and getting the whole family involved.

Even though he might not be as sharp or agile as a little puppy, your older Shorkie still has that built-in desire to please you. Puppies are known for their short attention span, but older dogs are actually easier to train because they can focus longer. However, an older Shorkie will need a little extra motivation and patience than a puppy, especially if he came from a home that mistreated him. If you adopted him from a shelter, they may be able to provide information about his past.

Rewards will keep your older dog motivated to keep trying to learn the new command or trick. If you need to correct bad behavior, such as chewing on the furniture or biting, then make sure you always have an appropriate chew toy on hand, and whenever he starts to chew on the furniture or bite, give him the chew toy. Once he starts chewing on the toy instead, praise him and reward him with a treat. It might take a while to reset years of bad habits, but with patience, he will slowly but steadily improve.

One of the biggest mistakes pet owners make while training an older dog is, they assume he has the energy level of a puppy. Mature adult dogs get tired faster than a puppy and might already have some health issues. How can you tell if your Shorkie is tired? Watch for any signs of exhaustion, such as excessive licking, being distracted, sniffing at the ground, yawning and dropping his ears.

Photo Courtesy of Beth Brehm

CHAPTER 4 Laying a Solid Foundation to Train Your Shorkie

Photo Courtesy of Kerry Harte

Here are some suggestions to consider when training an older dog:
- Keep training lessons fun and positive if you find yourself becoming agitated or nervous, then it is best to take a break.
- Recognize and take into consideration your adult dog's limitations.
- A loved and respected dog will more likely respond to your training than a dog that is fearful of his owner.
- Positive reinforcement is your secret weapon.
- Only work on one trick at a time; multiple tricks will only confuse and frustrate your dog.
- Try to change the location for each training session, so he associates the praise and reward with the command and not the place.

- Be patient - studies show that it can take four to eight weeks to teach an old dog new tricks.
- Keep the training sessions short and sweet.
- Start off using treats as a reward and as your dog improves, you can give him more praise and fewer snacks.

If your dog is elderly and has serious health conditions, learning something new might be too much for him. Training should be fun for both of you and an opportunity to help you bond with your dog. If your Shorkie's health or age prevents him from learning a new trick simply make him feel loved and cared for.

When to Call a Professional

If you start training your dog from the first day you bring him home, there really should not be any need to call in a professional dog trainer.

Honestly, no dog parent wants to have to call in the big dogs for help with their four-legged best friend. Yet, there are a few rare cases where you might need help no matter how embarrassed or disappointed you feel.

Biting – It is normal for a puppy to go through a biting phase when he is teething. However, we are referring to when a dog is aggressive towards just about anything that moves by viciously biting or snapping at them. Aggression cannot be fixed by an average person. Your dog will need help from a professional dog trainer who specializes in behavioral issues.

Separation anxiety – Separation anxiety is normal for smaller breeds such as Shorkies, but there are ways to reprogram that bad behavior. If you have tried and tried and your dog still goes into panic mode when left home alone even for thirty minutes, then he might need specialized training and medication to help him stay calm when left alone.

BOTTOM LINE: If you find you don't have the patience, personality or ability to properly train your dog, do not feel ashamed to ask for professional help.

CELEBRITY SHORKIES
Josephine Baker

American actress Kerry Washington is the proud owner of a Shorkie named Josephine Baker, or Josie B for short. Josie has appeared in photo shoots in several magazines, including People, Vogue, and In Style. You can see her and her mom enjoying some snuggles on Kerry Washington's Instagram (@kerry-washington), or you can follow Josie on Twitter (@JosietheShorkie)!

CHAPTER 4 Laying a Solid Foundation to Train Your Shorkie

Unacceptable Behavior from Day One

Have you ever asked yourself: "Why does my dog do that?"
The truth is: Dogs will be dogs!

Often, the behaviors we consider to be inappropriate for our dog are just normal parts of their personality and are considered typical canine behavior. For example, they love to chew on sticks, bones and basically anything else that fits in their mouth. Dogs bark, they dig, they fetch and do a long list of doggy behavior. Many of these behaviors we consider to be bad are actually innate to your dog, such as the barking and digging.

Photo Courtesy of Liz and Karl Machin

If you punish a dog for something that is part of his natural instinct, he most likely will not understand. The only way to correct these deep, ingrained behavioral traits is by using positive reinforcement of good behavior rather than punishment of bad behavior.

Here are some common behavioral issues that need to be nipped in the bud before they turn into a problem for you and your neighbors.

Chewing

All dogs love to chew, especially puppies as they explore their new world by biting on different objects - including your feet. Puppies chew on everything to help soothe their sore, swollen gums as they are teething. However, this behavior can turn into a habit if they are not taught what items are appropriate for chewing and what is not.

Simple solution: Doggy proof your house, have loads of suitable chew toys on hand and place your puppy in a safe place when you cannot supervise him.

Excessive Barking

All dogs naturally bark. Nonetheless, excessive barking is unacceptable as it will give you a headache, and it may upset your neighbors. If your Shorkie is barking for your attention, ignore him until he stops barking; then, reward him with treat for being quiet. Never yell at him to hush up as he will think you are telling him to bark more. If he is barking at a stranger, tell him it is ok and introduce him to the new person, reassuring him there is no reason to be scared.

Digging

All dogs love to dig no matter their size or breed. Shorkies are not much for digging twigs or bones, but on a hot summer day, they might be tempted to dig up your flower garden to find a nice, cool place to have a siesta. If your pup will be spending time outside unsupervised, you might want to consider getting a small fence to prevent him from digging up your tulips.

Separation Anxiety

Separation anxiety happens when your dog goes crazy when left alone, whether by barking, chewing, whining, etc. Get help from a family member who is hiding somewhere nearby but can listen to your dog. Place your Shorkie in his crate or confinement area with a chew toy and leave. When you come back, if he behaved himself, greet him calmly and reward his good behavior. Each time make your time away a little longer, until he learns how he is supposed to act when he is home alone.

CHAPTER 4   Laying a Solid Foundation to Train Your Shorkie

Running away

Your Shorkie's heredity genes are programmed to sniff out a small rodent or animal, so do not surprised when his little nose gets him in trouble! If you have a fenced back yard, get down on your knees (at your dog's height) to make sure you see no spaces that he can squeeze under and escape. If you do not have a fence, then keep him tied up when outside and unsupervised.

Jumping up

Dogs often jump on their human family or guests because they are excited. Giving a firm "no" or "get down", might even get your dog more excited, and he might start jumping up even more. Do

Photo Courtesy of Ciarra Owens

not acknowledge your dog until he is standing on all four paws, then calmly greet your dog. If he continues jumping up, turn around so your back is facing the dog; when he calms down, then praise and reward your dog. Trust me - it really works!

Begging

Begging is a habit that is learned, so it is also quite easy to prevent. When it is time for you and your family to enjoy dinner, just place your pup in his crate or confinement area.

Most bad behavior is an indication your pup is bored, has excessive energy or is overly tired.

CHAPTER 5
Everything You Need to Know About Housetraining

You should be prepared and equipped to start house training your Shorkie before you bring him home. In this chapter, you will learn all of the skills and methods needed to successfully housetrain your dog. Puppies must be trained from scratch, and if you adopt an adult dog from a shelter, he will need to have his memory refreshed.

Housetraining your dog requires consistency, patience and positive reinforcement. It involves more than just teaching him where to go to the bathroom but also showing your Shorkie how to let you know when he needs to go to the bathroom and what an appropriate location looks like.

Photo Courtesy of Sarah Horwath

CHAPTER 5   Everything You Need to Know About Housetraining

Photo Courtesy of Lizette Fitzpatrick

Crate Training Basics

Many pet owners might think confining their dog to small crate is inhumane and cruel. However, the dog considers the crate to be his private room with a view or a safe haven. Dogs in general prefer small, confined spaces as it makes them feel secure.

The majority of breeders, trainers and veterinarians highly recommend crate training your dog. Crate training is essential for housebreaking any type of dog as they are reluctant to soil their sleeping quarters. Dogs teach themselves to hold their bladder while inside of the crate, meaning less messes for you to clean up.

The crate becomes your Shorkie's private retreat where he can run whenever he feels he needs a break or wants to have a nap. He can run to his crate when he is frightened by noises like fireworks, thunder or even a baby crying. Crate training your dog is also a huge plus for when you need to travel long-distances, either by car or plane.

Benefits of crate training your Shorkie:

- Keeps your curious Shorkie safe when you are unable to supervise him

- Helps strengthen his bladder and bowel muscles as Shorkies instinctively will try to keep their sleeping quarters clean
- Creates a safe haven for your dog from rambunctious children or other disturbances that might stress or frighten him
- Makes transporting your dog to the groomer or vet and traveling in general easier

Although crate training is a fantastic training tool, it can be abused. Never leave your Shorkie locked inside of the crate all day long as leaving a dog locked inside for long periods at a time is inhumane and cruel. This can cause emotional distress or destructive behavior, not to mention physical harm.

If you have to work or will be gone all day, hire a dog sitter or ask a friend to drop by every few hours to let your Shorkie out of his crate to play, to stretch and to go the bathroom.

Regular maintenance of your Shorkie's crate is required. Otherwise, it can become soiled and become a breeding ground for bacteria. To prevent this, regularly wash your Shorkie's bedding in hot water and disinfect his crate with pet-friendly cleaning supplies.

Remove any harnesses, dangling ID tags and collars that could get caught on the crate doors to avoid injury or accidental strangulation.

Photo Courtesy of Nancy Forsythe

CHAPTER 5   Everything You Need to Know About Housetraining

How to Crate Train

Before we begin, here are some suggestions on where to place your pup's new private bedroom.

- Choose a quiet area, avoiding busy high traffic areas such as hall-ways or entrances
- Do not place the crate near a fireplace, radiator, heating or cooling vents or in direct sunlight
- Place the crate inside a play pen, making sure there are no power cords or poisonous houseplants your dog can access
- Place the crate close enough to your bedroom, so you can hear your Shorkie at night if he needs to go potty

Before you put your Shorkie into his crate, make sure he has had an opportunity to go to the bathroom and to burn off excess energy. Once he goes into his crate, praise him and reward him with a treat.

Never force your dog into the crate! When you introduce him to the crate, let him go inside on his own terms. Place warm, cozy blankets inside the crate and leave the door wide open. Throw in a few yummy treats to coax your Shorkie inside to explore. Do not close the door once he goes inside.

You want your dog to associate positive memories with his crate, so if he is wary about entering the crate, place his food dish inside of the crate by the door. Once he feels comfortable, push the food dish further towards the back of the crate and try closing the door until he has finished eating. When he finally embraces his crate, you can place his food dish elsewhere.

Once your Shorkie is comfortable entering and exiting the crate, persuade your puppy to go inside the crate with a few treats or with his favorite toy and close the door for fifteen to thirty. Then, let him out for a few seconds and generously praise him.

Encourage him to re-enter his crate. Repeat this action two or three times; then reward your Shorkie by playing

FUN FACT
Doggy DNA Tests

DNA tests have become increasingly popular in recent years, and now they're even available for your dog. These tests can give you a better understanding of your dog's genetic makeup, and some dog owners have been surprised by the results. Phyllis Von Saspe of New York owned a dog named Emma, who she believed was a Shorkie. Von Saspe supposedly purchased Emma from a breeder in Washington State, but when she ran a DNA test, she found out that Emma was actually half Yorkie and half Pomeranian.

with him. Slowly build up to longer time periods, until your dog is comfortable with staying inside with the door closed for around fifteen minutes.

More suggestions to consider during this step:
- Take your time and never leave your dog's side during the crate training sessions
- If your pup is happily engaged with his chew toy instead of barking or whining, you know the training sessions are working
- If your Shorkie struggles to stay calm, increase the rewards to motivate him a little more and decrease the time inside the crate with the door shut. Praise him and talk to him in a consoling voice while petting him inside of the crate
- This isn't competition, so go slowly and adapt to your dog's speed

Once your Shorkie will comfortably stay inside of the crate for fifteen minutes with the door shut and with you sitting beside the crate, start to move away from the crate each training session. Try closing the door and walking to the middle of the room, etc. Repeat this until you are able to walk outside of the room without your dog feeling stressed.

Slowly increase the time and begin to do activities around the house so your Shorkie is aware you are nearby but doing something. If he becomes agitated or stressed, reduce the time again and slowly increase it until he is comfortable being left inside of his crate.

Once your dog is comfortable with being left in the crate for fifteen minutes at a time, you can start leaving him inside for longer periods of time. If he is still a puppy and not housebroken, never leave him inside his crate for more than thirty minutes at time. A fully-grown dog that is house-trained should never be left inside of his crate for more than four hours at a time.

Do's and don'ts of crate training:
- Never punish your dog while he is inside the crate, otherwise he will associate his crate with negative experiences.
- Never leave your dog inside the crate for more than four hours at time. Crates are NOT substitute dog sitters. Leaving them locked inside can cause separation anxiety and depression.
- Do not make a big show over your departure. Place your dog inside the crate a few minutes before leaving and make sure he is occupied with a toy or treat before you leave.
- Do take your dog to the bathroom as soon as you get home, as this will help your dog realize potty time comes after crate time.

CHAPTER 5 Everything You Need to Know About Housetraining

Photo Courtesy of Andrew Warren

Housetraining Basics

Housetraining is not as intimidating of a task as you might imagine. All you need is the right attitude, commitment and consistency on your part.

Indoor potty-training is the best viable option for smaller dog breeds, such as your Shorkie, and even more so if you live in an apartment building, have restricted access to an enclosed yard or live in colder climates. The following guidelines are also viable for outdoor potty-training. Here are the following steps to get started:

Restrict your dog's movements inside of your house: Place him in his play pen or enclosed area. If he starts displaying signs he needs to go to the bathroom, say a key word, such as "potty" and pick him up and take him to his pad. Once he has finished, praise him and reward his good behavior. Do not allow your dog to freely roam about your house until he is housebroken. If he soils himself outside of his designated bathroom area, he will return to that area to go the bathroom.

Do not acknowledge bad behavior: If your Shorkie has an accident, simply take him to his pad or litter box. Never yell at him or tell him he is a bad dog or give him another type of punishment. Clean up his mess using an enzyme-based cleaner. Remind yourself the reason your dog had an accident is because you were not paying attention to his signs when he needed to go to the bathroom.

Follow a feeding schedule: If your dog eats twice a day, I recommend placing his food dish on the floor next to his water bowl. Let him enjoy his meal for fifteen to twenty minutes, then remove his dish regardless if he finished or not. This will teach him he needs to eat when its mealtime.

Establish a training room: If you have to go out or are unable to supervise your Shorkie for a few hours, place him in a small room like the bathroom. Place pads all over the floor, with his crate, bedding and water dish. Each day remove a pad, until there is only one pad left. If he soils himself off the pads or newspaper, then start gain by placing pads all over the floor.

Take your dog to the designated bathroom area every few hours: I recommend setting an alarm every two to three hours to remind yourself to take him to his bathroom spot. Also, take your dog whenever your Shorkie wakes up, after playtime, training sessions, eating or before naptime. When he goes, generously praise him and reward him with a treat. If he does not seem interested in going, wait five minutes and then move him back to his playpen.

Nighttime: Just because it is bedtime does not mean you can take a break from housetraining. Take turns with a family member to get up every hour or two to take your puppy to the bathroom. Remember, his bladder is not fully developed yet, and he will not be able to hold it all night.

CHAPTER 5 Everything You Need to Know About Housetraining

Photo Courtesy of Amanda Halstead

Try to maintain this routine for two to three weeks. If your dog stops having accidents in the house, you can start giving him a little more freedom each week. Reinforce good behavior by continually rewarding him for using his litter box or pad.

*If you are planning on housetraining your dog to mostly go to the bathroom outside, follow the above method but emphasize on going to the bathroom in a designated spot outside.

Photo Courtesy of Jensen Joe

Potty pads vs. Litter box

Potty pads or a litter box are extremely convenient as they provide your Shorkie with a legitimate bathroom spot inside of the house. You will need to teach your dog to use them as he will not have a natural desire to eliminate on or in them.

Litter boxes – Litter boxes can be filled with odorless doggy litter, and it is relatively easy to clean up. Such boxes have raised sides, which prevent urine or stool from spilling onto your floor. Dog litter is preferable to cat litter as it is made of larger bits and absorbs more urinary volume. The main disadvantage to this option is smaller dogs may be hesitant to crawl into a litter box, making housetraining more challenging.

Grass pads – Grass pads resemble a litter box but with artificial turf that mimics the outside. Like litter boxes, they have raised sides to prevent urine from leaking on the floor. This option can be helpful if you are housetraining your puppy to go outside, as it will help reinforce positive bathroom surfaces. On the other hand, the grass pads need to be regularly cleaned otherwise they become quite smelly.

Potty pads – Potty pads are super absorbent, disposable or washable pads that protect your floors. Some pads come with a scent that entices your dog to use it as a bathroom. The lack of edges means there will be the occasional spillage. The main disadvantage is it can be messy if you do not replace the pad with a new one before saturation occurs.

Whether you choose a litter box, artificial turf or potty pads, you will need to train your dog to use it by literally taking him to the designated spot. Reinforce good behavior by praising him each time he goes in the right place. Be patient and never punish him.

When housetraining relapses:

It can be disheartening to discover your housebroken dog regressing to bad bathroom behavior. However, before you throw in the towel there are some valid reasons your Shorkie's housetraining may have started to unravel:

- **Health** – Medical issues, like a urinary infection might be the underlying reason behind his accidents. Before assuming that your dog is having behavioral issues get your veterinarian to rule out any physical problems.

- **New environment** – Just because your dog is housebroken in your house, does not guarantee he will know how to act when placed in a new setting. If you are traveling or visiting a friend's house, go back to basic housetraining methods until you can trust your Shorkie again.

- **Climate changes** – Be proactive by watching your dog's potty habits, during the warmer months as he might be outside more and might

need to be gently reminded of proper indoor bathroom etiquette as the weather changes.
- **Hormonal behavior** – As your Shorkie matures, he will have hormonal changes. Marking territory is a common behavior trait for both male and female dogs. If your dog is marking inside of the house, then return to the first steps of housetraining. In case the problems persist, you can consider using a belly-band designed to prevent him from marking.

A belly band for dogs looks like a big band-aid or diaper that wraps around your Shorkie's rear girth. Often, the belly ban has a waterproof shell with an absorbent liner which prevents any unwanted accidents in your house. Most styles are reusable and machine washable.
- **Fear or anxiety** – Loud noises, such as construction, thunderstorms, music, etc. can cause your dog to become frightened or even traumatized. If this happens, try to isolate the sound that startled him and reinforce good memories in that area.

Involuntary urination:

Involuntary urination or defecation is not a housetraining issue, as your dog simply has no control over it and is unaware he just soiled himself. Here are some common reasons for involuntary urination:
- **Excitement** – Younger dogs will involuntarily urinate when they are overly excited or overjoyed to see someone. To avoid this happening, downplay greetings by only casually greeting your dog. Try walking in and throwing his favorite chew toy to distract him, only greeting your Shorkie once he has calmed down.
- **Incontinence** – Age or sickness can cause urinary or fecal incontinence, causing your dog to feel an urge to potty while sleeping or playing. In this case follow any recommendations of your veterinarian and use a belly-belt (doggy diaper) to reduce cleanup.

Signs your Shorkie needs to go the bathroom:

You can tell when your Shorkie has to go to the bathroom by learning to read his body language. By being attentive, you will learn to understand when he needs to go pee or poop. The following telltale signs will help prevent accidents:
- **Sniffing the floor** – Dogs will sniff out an area to go potty and will, look for a familiar scent. If your Shorkie starts sniffing the floor or around your furniture, immediately take him to his designated area and praise him for going potty there.
- **Turning in circles while sniffing the floor** – Sniffing the floor might just mean your pup is searching for something to eat. If he starts turning

CHAPTER 5 Everything You Need to Know About Housetraining

around in circles while sniffing, however, then he probably has to poop. Pick him up as fast as you can and get him to his spot. Again, praise him for a job well done.

- **Barking, scratching or standing at the door** – Puppies generally are very vocal about when they need to go. If he starts barking and staring in the direction of the door or his pee pads, then take him out immediately.

- **Whining** – If whining is combined with any of the above behaviors, your dog most likely needs to go potty. Younger dogs that still have not mastered housebreaking will often just sit there and cry to tell you they need to go really badly.

Photo Courtesy of Hazel Esguerra

Cleaning up after your Shorkie

It is inevitable your Shorkie will have an accident in the house, no matter how careful and diligent the training methods. When this happens, you need to clean-up those accidents quickly, efficiently and correctly.

This is because if you do not properly clean and deodorize where your puppy had an accident, it will lead to more accidents in the same area. Simply wiping up the mess, might satisfy your eyes and nose, but there is enzymatic scent only your dog can smell that will lure him back to the same spot later on.

For any type of accident, pick up any solids with a paper towel or baggy and blot up any excess liquid. Avoid using any ammonia-based cleaning products as it may enhance the urine smell, which will make the spot irresistible for your puppy.

The best cleaning products will not mask the scent or simply clean up the accident, but they will neutralize the enzymes that entice your dog to pee or poop in that same spot. Look for products that are specifically designed for cleaning up after pets.

Rewarding Positive Behavior

Rewarding positive behavior is the preferred training method by trainers and breeders worldwide. However, it is not simply about praising your dog every time he does something that pleases you. If you want to successfully housetrain your Shorkie there are few do's and don'ts you should follow.

Do....
Praise and reward good behavior immediately – Your Shorkie has a very short memory, so if he does something worth praising, then do so immediately. This way he will be able to associate the good behavior with affection, praise and sometimes delicious treats.

Wean away from treats – Treats are an excellent method in the beginning to teach your pup proper behavior, but with time you should wean him off treats and replace them with praise and rewards. This is essential with older dogs as they do not need the extra calories.

Don't....
Punish your dog – Your dog will try to please you but he will make mistakes and get distracted. If he has a potty accident, do not yell at him or hit him. Just clean up the mess and get on with your life.

CHAPTER 5   Everything You Need to Know About Housetraining

When to Use a Playpen

A doggy playpen is a wonderful tool for keeping your Shorkie safe, secure, engaged and near to you! Getting a new dog is a full-time job, and nobody expects you to keep an eye on him 24/7. A playpen encloses an area of your house, so your dog has the freedom to roam about and play without getting himself into trouble. Plus, it is a huge asset in housetraining your Shorkie, but there are certain points to consider before you buy a playpen for your pup.

- **Durable materials** – You want a pen that is durable enough to withstand some chewing and strong enough to prevent your puppy from pushing his way out.
- **Size and height** – It should be tall enough so he cannot jump or crawl out of it. If it comes with interlocking panels to expand or change the shape of the pen, that will factor in the full-grown size of your Shorkie, this allows you to use the playpen throughout his life.
- **Easy set-up** – You will be moving the playpen from room to room when you are housetraining your Shorkie. For this reason, it needs to be portable and easy to set up.

When choosing a playpen for your dog, take into consideration the layout of your home. Most outdoor playpens can be used inside but the opposite is not always possible. Consider portability if you want to travel with your playpen or use it outside during the warmer months.

CHAPTER 6
Socializing Your Shorkie

Socialized dogs are less likely to develop behavior issues as the grow up. Socializing your dog involves making him feel comfortable in new surroundings, around new smells, new people and other animals. Positive experiences with new situations, people and animals will have a direct impact on how he will accept a similar experience later in his life.

Younger Shorkies are quick to accept whatever they encounter in their environment until they reach a certain age. Once they are fully-grown they naturally start to become suspicious of anything new they have not experienced yet. Adult dogs that have not be properly socialized during their younger years often will be fearful or aggressive when exposed to something new.

Photo Courtesy of Dyanne Letts

CHAPTER 6   Socializing Your Shorkie

Why Socialize Your Shorkie?

The best time to start socializing your Shorkie is between three weeks to six months. After that age, he will start to become much more suspicious and cautious around anything he has never encountered. After that time period, it becomes more of a challenge to get him to accept a new situation that he finds scary.

Well-socialized dogs are generally more enjoyable to be around. They often have fewer health issues and outlive other dogs that are constantly stressed out by their surroundings. This is unlike poorly socialized dogs which often react aggressively or fearfully when presented with a new situation, such as cats, honking horns, postmen, veterinary visits, crowds or even elevators.

The more experiences your dog is exposed to the better!

Socialization is a planned project. Take into consideration the type of sounds, people, places and experiences your dog will encounter during his life. Make a list of any sights or sounds he will be exposed to, such as garbage trucks, trains, a schoolyard full of screaming children, cats, livestock, crying babies, etc. Make it your goal to get your Shorkie used to the common type of people, objects, noises and physical handling that will be part of his daily life.

> **SOCIAL MEDIA SHORKIES**
> **Bella the Shorkie**
>
> Bella is an Instagram celebrity from Charlotte, NC, and has over nine thousand followers on the social media platform. She was born on December 10, 2017, and is the spokespet for Bella Boutique and Co., an independent shop specializing in handmade accessories for dogs. You can find Bella on Instagram with the username @bellatheshorkie.

When socializing your Shorkie try the following:
- Expose him to only one new situation at a time. For example, if you plan on socializing with other puppies, do it in a park with which he is already familiar.
- Following a new experience, always use positive reinforcement by giving generous praise, petting and of course, treats.
- If your Shorkie is frightened of a new experience, such as hearing a group of children playing in the park, sit further away and gradually move closer each time. Make sure the experience is positive every time by offering treats and some playtime with you.

Socialization is not an option but an essential element in helping your Shorkie develop into a relaxed and fun companion. It will be easier to share your life with him if he is well-adjusted, gets along with other people and animals and adapts quickly to new situations.

Introducing Your New Puppy to Other Dogs

One of the best ways to socialize your puppy with other dogs is by attending puppy classes. Often, they are referred to as kindergarten classes for puppies because they teach them how to socialize with other dogs. A typical class will teach your dog how to play gently with other dogs and to becomes used to being petted and handled by other people. Another advantage of these classes is they will teach your Shorkie some general obedience skills.

Since your Shorkie has not received all of his vaccinations at this age, you should be careful when exposing your puppy to unknown animals or even walking in areas where animals might have been. However, if you wait to socialize your dog until he is old enough to be vaccinated, you might miss out on vital training opportunities.

By taking the following precautions when socializing your puppy, you almost completely eliminate the risks of him becoming sick:

- Socialize your Shorkie in a controlled environment such as indoors or a backyard that can easily be disinfected. Avoid socializing in dog parks or other areas with a lot of unfamiliar dogs.
- If socializing your puppy with a friend's dog ask if his vaccinations are up-to-date and if he is parasite-free before doing a meet-and-greet.
- Sign up for puppy classes that specialize in socializing younger dogs.
- Daily walks are great opportunities to expose your dog to other dogs, plus it will burn off excess energy. Word of caution: before introducing

CHAPTER 6 Socializing Your Shorkie

your Shorkie to a dog while on your walk, ask the dog owner if their dog's vaccinations are up-to-date and if they are parasite-free.

If you adopted an older dog or were unable to socialize your Shorkie when he was younger, you can still teach an old dog new tricks.

For example, if you have an older dog, take him to the dog park, but instead of letting him lose and praying for the best, start off by walking him around the park on his leash for a week or two without letting him become too excited. Allow him to act as an observer until he is ready for the next step. Then, gradually walk inside the park until your Shorkie can calmly approach new dogs.

Photo Courtesy of Susan Massoni

Socializing with Other Pets

Bringing a new puppy home is thrilling and exciting for you, but your other household pets might not share your joy. Choose a neutral space for their first encounter, such as your backyard or the entrance to your house. Stay calm and do not punish your older dog for any negative reactions.

Some practical tips for a smooth first introduction:
- Choose a time when your older pet is most relaxed and calm, such as after playtime or eating.
- Introduce the new dog while he is on a leash; this will allow the older pet to feel as if he is in control of the situation.
- Focus on your older pet by giving him some of his favorite snacks.
- Once your new pet seems like he might accept the new dog, take the two of them into the house together.
- If you are concerned about the safety of your new Shorkie, place his crate inside the playpen until you can ensure the safety of the new puppy
- If there any altercations between the two of them, do not become annoyed with your older pet. It is perfectly normal that the older dog will try to put the new dog in his place. Stay calm and let them establish who is the boss.

Small puppies can be quite annoying for older pets, and they could feel a tad-bit jealous of the new dog. Be sure to coddle your old house pets with extra love and attention, otherwise they might be even more stand-offish to the new dog. Do not expect them to embrace the new dog quickly; sometimes it can take up to six months before the new addition to the household is accepted.

Plus, some helpful suggestions to ease the tension:
- Confine the new dog to a certain part of the house that is far away from the older pet's feeding and bathroom area. Make any changes needed a week or two before bringing home the new dog.
- Place the new dog in his crate and place the crate near to the older pet – only after your current pet has finished eating or his play time. This will ensure he remains, calm and relaxed, and will allow your older pet to investigate the new dog on his own terms.
- Give the older pet the royal treatment, so his feelings will not be hurt. Do not let the new dog push past him for your affection or praise. Give your older resident pet priority!

CHAPTER 6   Socializing Your Shorkie

Cats and Dogs

The old phrase "fighting like cats and dogs" tends to be true when the cat and dog have not been properly socialized. According to the American Veterinary Medical Association, almost 50% of pet owners in the United States have multiple pets. Since the most common combination are cats and dogs, how can you help them get along?

If you are introducing the new dog to a resident cat, you will need to give your cat more space. Most cats will wait for the new dog to approach them and then give them a quick bat on the nose, which will teach your Shorkie to have a deep respect for the cat. Avoid overreacting as this will make your cat even more sensitive to the new intruder inside of his house.

> **HELPFUL TIP**
> **How to Know When Socialization Is Needed**
>
> Socialization is an important part of every dog's life, but how can you tell when your dog is not being or has not been socialized enough? Signs that your Shorkie needs more socialization training include cowering, running away, hiding, and nervous behavior such as trembling and shaking. Sometimes your Shorkie may display aggressive behaviors that are rooted in fear, such as growling or excessive barking.

Do not be surprised if there are altercations between the two of them. If the cat growls or bats his paws at the dog, it his way of communicating his boundaries to the dog. With time, the cat will learn to coexist with the new dog… so no need to worry!

Just as you would with your older resident dog, reassure your cat you love him by petting him and giving him some of his favorite snacks. Cats like to do things on their own terms so never force your cat to meet-and-greet the new dog as it will not end well.

Realize your cat has a definite personality. If he acts like he just barely tolerates the new dog then that means that he probably has accepted your Shorkie.

The following steps will maximize the chances for success:
- Prepare a dog-free sanctuary for your cat that she can access at all times. Place all of your cat's essential items inside of the "safe", room such as her litter box, water and food dishes, scratching post and toys. If you cannot create a dog-free zone for your cat, place his litter box and scratching post up high and out of the reach of your Shorkie.
- Set up hiding spots for your cat throughout the house, such as tunnels or objects she can hide behind or allow her access to high areas so she can perch and observe the new dog from a comfortable distance.

- Be prepared to supervise your pets' interactions for at least the next few weeks, perhaps even longer.
- Before you bring home your Shorkie, make sure your cat is up-to-date with her vaccinations and is parasite-free. Plan to keep your pets separated for at least three-days after the new arrival. The goal is for your cat to get used to your dog's presence without face-to-face contact. Even though they cannot see each other, they can smell and hear each other.
- Feed them on opposite sides of a closed door. This will help your cat to associate the presence of the new dog with something pleasant such as eating. If your cat seems skittish about eating close to the door, then place her food dish a few feet away and slowly move it closer each day or until your cat is comfortable eating next to the door.
- Begin face-to-face meetings in the common area of your house. Keep your Shorkie on a leash and distracted with a chew toy and let your cat come and go as she wishes. Do not restrain either pet as that could result in injury. Reward your cat with treats and praise and then do the same with your dog. If either pet shows signs of aggression, redirect your pet's attention by tossing a play toy, etc.

Socializing with other animals

Do you have other pets, such as geckos, hamsters, guinea pigs, rabbits, gerbils, etc.?

Dogs in general consider small animals as prey. Before you introduce your small critters to your Shorkie, it will come in handy if your dog has already learned some basic commands such as "Sit" "Come", and "Stay." These commands will help your dog to be well-mannered and to make a good impression on your other house pets.

Before their initial introduction, take your Shorkie outside for a walk around the block or a game of fetch in the backyard. A hyperactive and excited pup can frighten your pet.

Keep your small critter confined for the first encounter. If your Shorkie does not show any signs of aggression, then let them run about their enclosure freely while your dog observes on his leash. Once your dog does not show any interest in chasing after them or any signs of aggression, let him off the leash. Never forget to praise and reward your dog for his good behavior around your other pets.

Remember Shorkies are half Yorkshire Terrier, who were originally bred to hunt small animals. A small animal such as a rabbit, hamster or guinea pig is an almost irresistible temptation, even more so if they begin run. Never leave your Shorkie unsupervised for long periods when near your small critter as he could accidently injure your pet.

CHAPTER 6   Socializing Your Shorkie

What if Your Pets Don't Get Along?

Every pet owner's dream is that their pets get along with each other, even snuggle up together while sleeping. Yet, the reality is pets do not always get along, especially if they are not the same species. If two pets just cannot seem to get along, they might need to be separated for a short time.

Why do they not get along?

Hormonal – Some disagreements could be related to hormonal changes. To avoid this, make sure all of the resident pets are spayed or neutered. This will keep any unwanted aggression at bay.

Food – All animals have a built-in instinct to protect their food. If they are showing aggression around meal times, try placing their food dishes in separate parts of the house.

Jealousy – Pets need to feel loved and cherished. An easy solution for this problem is to designate a special, consistent bonding time with each pet alone.

Dominance – Rivalry among animals is normal, as only one of them can be the leader of the pack, and this something they need to figure out on their own terms and on their own time schedule. Once it has been established which pet is the boss, respect their decision by feeding the leader first, etc.

If a fight does break out, never try to separate the animals as you might become injured. The best solution is dousing them with water. Never punish your pets as it will only make the problem worse. Try to keep them separated and supervised until they learn to behave together.

If they start fighting while on a walk, redirect their attention to something else and continue on the walk. Reward them once they are calm and submissive. Eventually, they will learn it benefits them both to get along with each other.

A good relationship between your pets might take a couple of days to few years to build.

If your pets continue to attack one another, even after extensive training, then they will need to separated permanently. Some pets cannot and will not tolerant other pets and are happier living in an "only child" household.

If you have to separate your pets, ensure the safety of your pet's future by finding him a loving new home. Every pet deserves to be loved and cherished. Attempt to personally hand-pick a new family for your pet. Be open and honest to the adoptive family regarding why your pet needs a new home; do not conceal any information about your dog. If possible, follow up on your pet's new family and surroundings after the adoption.

Shorkies and Strangers

Even the friendliest dog can become aggressive. Your Shorkie needs to be exposed to as many different types of people as possible, but the quantity of those experiences is not as important as the quality of each one. He needs to associate the new person with the idea of it being a new and fun experience.

Avoid being nervous or stressed out when taking your dog out of his comfort zone. Dogs are very observant and can read our emotions. If we are nervous, then our dog will be nervous, too, and they might even become fearful of the new experience.

Take baby steps. There is no need for him to meet everyone on your list in a few days, otherwise you will just overwhelm your Shorkie. Start off slowly, first with friends and relatives then integrate a stranger, - such as postman. Avoid taking him to busy public areas as he could easily become frightened and become fearful of strangers in general.

Before you take your dog to meet a new person, inform them you will be bringing your Shorkie over for a socialization session. Ask them to be ready to pamper him with love and maybe a treat or two.

Start off with meeting new people in safe environments, such as on the street while going for a walk, in your yard, at a friend's house or inside of a small store. Once he has climatized to these situations, try something more adventurous, such as outside of a shopping center with more people.

Expose him to a wide variety of people, from women to men of all sizes. Introduce him to people wearing different types of clothes, such as uniforms, hats, sunglasses, etc.

Suggestions to help him become acclimated to all sorts of people - not just you and your family:

- Be calm and confident during the meet-and-greet. If your dog gets scared, do not make a big deal out of it.
- Ask new people to pet your dog on his chest or under his chin. That way, he will be able to see where they are putting their hand, which will reduce skittish behavior.
- Use positive reinforcement each time your dog meets a new person by giving him a treat or praise.
- Hire a different dog-sitter or dog-walker each week, so he is exposed to a large variety of people.

CHAPTER 6   Socializing Your Shorkie

Photo Courtesy of Lori Laabs

Your Shorkie should be exposed to the following list of people within his first six months:
- Neighbors
- Family and friends
- Unfamiliar people wearing different styles of clothes (hooded jackets, sunglasses, hats, jackets)
- Groomer and vet
- Postman
- Anyone who regularly comes to your house

When planning these encounters choose a variety of different environments for each encounter, such as urban centers, parks, vehicles, etc. Let your dog investigate foreign objects, such as street signs, bicycles, skateboards, strollers and benches.

Be sure to follow your Shorkies cues. Make interactions short and sweet. You want him to become acquainted with a new person without wearing your dog out.

Shorkies and Children

Socializing your Shorkie with children is a must even if you don't have children of your own. Here is everything you need to know about socializing your dog with children of all ages:

Create a positive environment – Before you start, make sure everyone is in a good mood. Never force a meeting with a tired and cranky kid. That definitely is not the right moment to make a good first impression. If the child is overly excited or rowdy, wait till until he calms down – otherwise, your Shorkie will be scared.

Take it slow – Children tend to make jerky movements and have louder voices, especially when they get excited, which can easily frighten your Shorkie. Before the meet-and-greet, instruct them regarding how to walk, talk and approach your dog. Tell them to use gentle hands when petting him and not to squeeze, pull, grab or poke at the puppy. Keep the introduction short and sweet.

Supervise – Smaller dogs, such as Shorkies, love children, but because of their small size they are fragile and not suited for rough play. Teach children how to gently pet your Shorkie. Never let them socialize with your dog without proper supervision. Never leave you dog alone with children!

Let your Shorkie set the pace – If your Shorkie is nervous around children, let him set the pace. Let him come to the children and choose

CHAPTER 6 Socializing Your Shorkie

his comfortable distance. Tell the kid to play with something and let the curious dog come and investigate. As his confidence grows, the child can pet him.

One of the disadvantages with children and puppies is they can easily get excited, which may cause misunderstandings and hurt feelings. Slow interactions will teach everyone how to behave around each other. It is important to teach your children that your Shorkie's crate is his private place; if he goes there, it is because he wants some down time.

Photo Courtesy of Kathy Thames

Steps for a successful first encounter with small children:
1. Have the child sit on the ground with their legs crossed. Place the puppy nearby and have the child place her hand out for the puppy to smell.
2. Once the puppy has sniffed out the little person, pick up your Shorkie and place him on the child's lap. Praise him and instruct the child to give him a treat. Then, the child can pet your dog using gentle strokes.
3. Your Shorkie might decide to cuddle up and go to sleep or decide to move on and investigate a little more. If the latter happens, tell the child not to pull on the puppy or drag him back. Doing so could hurt and frighten your tiny dog.
4. If your dog decides to explore his surroundings, let him walk around a few minutes. Then, redirect his attention back to the child by placing him once again on her lap. If he runs again, reassure the child the puppy does like her, and he is just very curious.
5. Maintain soft, calming voices and praise your dog every time he sits with the child. A positive experience will lay the foundation for a healthy friendship between children and your Shorkie.

Socializing your dog will be an ongoing process throughout his life. Never force interactions. Let him set his terms for discovering new situations, environments and people. Avoid loud voices that could startle your Shorkie. A properly socialized dog will feel comfortable around a wide variety of people, including large groups.

CHAPTER 7
Puppy-Parenting

Shorkies are beyond adorable, but let's be honest – raising a puppy is not without its challenges. If you have never had a dog or puppy before, the very thought of puppy parenthood can be quite daunting. Nonetheless, there is no turning back once those big brown eyes capture your heart! In this chapter, we will discuss how to help your Shorkie grow into a happy, healthy and well-adjusted dog.

Photo Courtesy of Sarah Keller

CHAPTER 7 Puppy-Parenting

Common puppy-parenting mistakes

Avoid these common mistakes, and you will raise an awesome dog.

Car rides – Is your Shorkie afraid of car rides? That might be because the only time he goes in the car is when he goes to the veterinarian's office to get pried and poked by strange people. Take your pup for car rides to fun places like the park, beach, pet store or doggy play-date at a friend's house. Praise your dog upon arriving at your destination and when you return home.

Forgetting to socialize – Take time to socialize your dog with other dogs. During the colder months, try to keep your Shorkie well-socialized with other dogs by organizing play-dates or by enrolling him in obedience classes.

Photo Courtesy of Steve and Jaime Adams

Table scraps – Your Shorkie's big brown eyes can melt even the coldest heart. Resist the temptation to feed him table scraps or people food of any kind. Once a dog learns to beg for food, it is one of the hardest behaviors to break that quickly gets out of control. Plus, human food is generally unhealthy for dogs and can cause future, digestive issues.

Lack of patience – Puppies grow fast! Your puppy is still discovering the world, and he will be a handful at times. Be patient. Adjusting to your new dog is not only a challenge for you but also your new pooch. He is in a new environment far away from his littermates and his mom.

Negative reactions – When housetraining your pup, it can be frustrating to come home and discover he had an accident on the carpet. Overreacting in these situations, either by scolding or yelling at your pup, will only confuse and frighten him. All he understands is that you are yelling at him. He already has forgotten about going potty. Be patient and remember he is still learning.

Punishing – When you hit your dog, you teach him to be afraid of you, and this is extremely harmful to his relationship with you. You are breaking a bond of trust and destroying his confidence. Hitting or punishing your dog will only create an insecure, fearful dog who will most likely lash out aggressively in the future.

Left alone for long periods – Dogs are pack animals. They thrive on being around people and other animals. If you must leave the house for long periods of time, consider hiring a doggy sitter or a daycare service that caters to dogs. Or, ask a close friend or relative to check in on your Shorkie

Photo Courtesy of Jennifer White

CHAPTER 7 Puppy-Parenting

and to give him a potty break and some love and affection. Never leave your dog alone for long periods of time.

Infrequent potty breaks Your puppy has little to no bladder control when you first bring him home. As much as he wants to please you by holding it in, he can't. Expecting him to wait hours between bathroom trips is impossible. Younger pups might need to go every thirty minutes. Do not let them wander around the house and simply hope for the best. Take time off to housetrain your dog... you won't regret it.

Not enough sleep – Puppies need plenty of sleep to stay happy, healthy and stimulated. When a puppy becomes over-tired or exhausted, he can become irritable, hyperactive and even aggressive. Puppies under the age of six months need an early bedtime and naptime in a safe, quiet designated sleep area.

Photo Courtesy of Lindsay Williams

How Do You Become the Alpha?

If you want an obedient dog, you need to establish yourself as the alpha leader. Most dogs, especially smaller breeds like the Shorkie, gravitate toward whoever is in charge. However, be aware the innocent Shorkie puppy will test your dominance before he decides to be submissive.

You set the rules and limitations – During the adolescent phase, your Shorkie will challenge you. He will try to define how far he can push his limits or his rules. Do not punish your dog; firmly correct the bad behavior, such as jumping up on the couch or grabbing a piece of food in your hand.

Be consistent – Decide on ground rules for the dog and make sure everyone respectfully follows them. If he starts chewing on your shoes, for example, quickly remove the shoe and say a firm, "NO." Then, replace

FUN FACT
Popularity

Since Shorkies are not yet recognized by the American Kennel Club (AKC), they aren't given a rank in the AKC's breed popularity list. Shorkies' parents, however, are! Yorkies are listed as the 10th most popular dog breed in America, according to the AKC, and Shih Tzus are ranked 20th.

it with an appropriate chew toy. Sometimes smaller dogs, like Shorkies, will whine until we pick them up. Do not pick your dog up until you have distracted him with another acceptable behavior.

Stay calm but be assertive – In nature, the leader of the pack, or the alpha dog, shows his dominance by taking charge of every situation. He is not nervous or doubtful. Your dog can sense your emotions. If you are uncertain or fearful, your Shorkie will interpret it as a sign of weakness. He will think he needs to protect you and to be your leader.

Never punish or physically hurt your dog to show him you are the alpha leader. Being the leader simply means you are there to protect him and you are the one who establishes - the rules. Keep in mind if you lose your patience and get angry with him, you will have already lost your position as the pack leader in the eyes of your Shorkie.

Consistency is Fundamental

The key to any type of training program is consistency. If you are not consistent, you will never see the results you want. Learning or changing behavioral patterns is altered by being able to identify new patterns.

In order for your Shorkie to understand what is expected of him, the entire family needs to be on the same page. If one person says, "Sit" and another says "Sit-down," your pup will be very confused, and it will take twice as long to teach him this command. If you are using nonverbal signs to indicate he should sit, make sure the whole family is aware of the sign.

Another reason to be consistent in your command cues is because your dog was not born understanding English. Even though he will quickly learn new words, he does not know that "Lie" and "Lie-down" have the same meaning. If one person tells him to "Come" and another says "Here," you cannot really expect him to understand. Consistency is fundamental.

Dogs love routine, and structure teaches them what to expect each day. Be consistent in feeding, walks, playtime and bathroom breaks. This will help him adapt to your daily schedule as it will become part of his routine, too.

CHAPTER 7 Puppy-Parenting

Photo Courtesy of Ashley Pesch

Clicker Training – It Really Works

A clicker is a small device you hold in your hand, which has a thin, metal strip inside that makes a distinctive clicking sound whenever you push down on the button. You can also download an app on your phone that duplicates the sound. Clicker training is often used with positive reinforcement training and is considered to be a highly, effective teaching method.

The clicking sound is faster than saying "Good Boy," and much more effective than training with treats (and healthier). You can find a clicker at any pet supply store, and they are quite inexpensive.

How to use a clicker:

1. Choose a calm area for training without any distractions, such as your backyard. Choose a moment when your dog is hungry, preferably before meals, to start clicker training Be sure to have a handful of treats in your hand or pocket.
2. First, you need to teach your Shorkie the meaning of a click. Click the device in your hand and immediately give your dog a treat and praise him generously.
3. Repeat this activity five to ten times each day until he associates the sound with the yummy reward.
4. Start using the clicker in training sessions to reinforce good behavior. Once your Shorkie learns the positive effects of the clicking sound, the noise starts acting as a reward in itself.
5. Once you and your dog have mastered clicker training, you can move on to more complicated commands and even tricks.

The clicking sound should not completely replace treats, but you will be able to wean him off treats, little by little. This method is especially handy if you are training an older Shorkie with weight or teeth issues. The clicking sound will register instantly with your dog and tell him he deserves an award. You will need to still give an occasional treat; otherwise, the clicker will lose its effectiveness.

If you are looking for a healthier option to doggy treats, you can give him smaller pieces of unseasoned cooked chicken or turkey during your clicker training sessions. Your dog lives in the moment, so when you click the clicker, immediately give him a treat, so he can associate the noise with a treat.

Test your Shorkie when he is distracted or not looking at you by clicking the clicker. If he quickly responds by looking at you and stopping whatever he is doing, then you know he is ready to be weaned off treats, little by little. If he does not respond to the sound, you know you need to spend more training sessions with the click-treat-combination until he is aware the sound means he will receive a reward.

CHAPTER 7   Puppy-Parenting

How to use the clicker for basic and advanced commands:

1. At the exact moment your Shorkie completes the desired action, press the clicker. Then, reward him with a treat and with praise.
2. Be aware that if you are not able to click at the exact moment your dog performed the new behavior, he might not associate the new action with the treat.
3. For more complicated commands or tricks, you can click and reward for small steps towards the desired behavior. For example, if you are teach-

Photo Courtesy of Andrew Warren

ing him to fetch the ball and bring it back to you, click for fetching and then again when your Shorkie brings the ball back.

One of the most common mistakes with clicker training is pet owners forget to give their dog verbal praise. Your Shorkie will associate the click sound with a reward, but he still needs your approval. Never ignore your pup's need for love and affection from you. This is especially important as dogs thrive on your praise.

Photo Courtesy of Anastasia Berglind

Mental Stimulation

One of the main factors for behavioral issues is boredom. When your dog is bored, he might start chewing on the furniture, digging up the garden or trying to escape your yard. Training sessions are an excellent way to keep your dog mentally stimulated. Learning new commands or tricks each day requires your dog's attention, which means he burns off the excess energy.

Keep training sessions fun and upbeat. Positive reinforcement will not only keep your Shorkie mentally stimulated, but it will create a special bond between the two of you.

> **STORY**
> **Doggy Rescue**
>
> In Hilton Head, SC, a little Shorkie named Coco survived a harrowing experience thanks to a two-year-old Golden Retriever named Tully. Coco wandered away from her home one night in the spring of 2020. She was missing for three days, during freezing temperatures. Multiple attempts to search for the 10-year-old pup were unsuccessful. That is until Tully found Coco shivering on the beach, three miles from home. Her survival was miraculous, and her owner, Gia King, was overjoyed to be reunited with her beloved pet.

In the beginning, he might have a hard time focusing or paying attention during his training sessions, but with time, he will view these teaching moments as playtime.

Mental stimulation enriches your Shorkie's life and helps to alleviate boredom and curb the development of behavioral issues, such as chewing or excessive barking.

Always keep your puppy busy:
- When you take your Shorkie for a walk, stop and let him sniff his surroundings. Walking might be a great physical exercise but exploring is very stimulating and exciting.
- Choose puzzle toys that allow you to place a piece of food inside. Your Shorkie will spend hours trying to get out that piece of food!
- Never underestimate the power of interactive playtime. Your Shorkie loves to play with you even if it is just tug-o-war or fetch.

Being a puppy parent and training your dog takes time, and you are surely going to have some ups and downs along the way. The key is your attitude – be positive, loving, patient and upbeat and your Shorkie will respond.

CHAPTER 8
Basic Commands

Many of the misunderstandings between dogs and humans are directly related to a communication gap. By teaching basic commands to your Shorkie, you are setting your dog up for a happy and safe life. Obedience training takes time; think of it as a marathon and not a short sprint. Some commands might be learned in a day or two, and others might take a few weeks to master.

Photo Courtesy of Nancy Serrano Vintimilla

CHAPTER 8 Basic Commands

Photo Courtesy of Regina Kellogg

Benefits of proper training

When a dog is constantly disobedient, it can be a source of stress for both you and your dog. Therefore, making sure your dog is well-trained is your responsibility; not just for your dog's benefit but for your own peace of mind as well. Your pup's behavior reflects directly on you as his owner. No matter the age of your Shorkie, he can benefit from obedience training.

Here are a few reasons why you need to train your dog:

- **Training benefits you and your dog** – When you train your dog, it is a win-win for the both of you. By working together to learn new commands and tricks, you will be able to comprehend your dog's personality and needs, which will make you a better puppy-parent. You and your dog will both benefit from the exercise, and the more behaved your pooch is, the easier it will be to take him along with you.
- **Training protects your Shorkie** – If you can control your dog with basic commands, it will be easier to control him when unrestrained. A disobedient dog could easily get hit by a car when off the leash or could slip out the front door just as you are leaving.
- **Training helps your dog be more sociable** – Obedience training helps your pup learn his boundaries and how to conduct himself in social

situations. People and other dogs will feel at ease around your dog. Positive interactions your dog has with strangers and other dogs will help your Shorkie to be more relaxed in new situations.

- **There is no age limit when training a dog** – Older dogs can learn new tricks. They simply might need more patience than a younger dog because of health problems or weight issues. It is never too late to improve your Shorkie's education. By doing so, he will experience less stress, be more sociable and form a stronger bond with you.

- **Training helps you when you need to travel** – Nobody enjoys being around a disobedient dog. A well-trained dog will obey just your commands as well as those of others. Training will make boarding a breeze, either at a kennel, close friend's house or a relative's home, when you have to travel.

The benefits of properly training your dog are endless. By taking the time to train your Shorkie you are making the best commitment to help him live the happiest, healthiest life possible. Plus, your Shorkie will be much more fun to be around.

Photo Courtesy of Cat Sullivan

CHAPTER 8 Basic Commands

Picking the Right Rewards/Treats

Photo Courtesy of Pauline Messier

There are many ways to reward your pup for his good behavior, but nothing is better than a yummy treat! Here are some useful tips to help you choose the best reward for different situations:

Small-sized treats – When you are teaching your Shorkie a new command or behavior it is important to keep him motivated and attentive. In these cases, he will be eating lots of treats in a short period of time. Choose treats that are smaller in size and that can be quickly gobbled up. If your dog spends too long chewing a treat between repetitions, maybe you will have to cut the treats in half.

Soft and smelly treats – All dogs love soft, stinky treats. These treats are best suited for more complex commands, such as "Leave it" or "Down." You might be able to get away with giving your pup a piece of kibble for training sessions in your living room, but in a public area with more distractions, he might need a little more motivation.

Chewy treats – For some training sessions, you need the treat to last longer, such as with crate training or learning to lie still beside you on the couch. For these occasions, use a chewy reward your pup can savor or try using a chewing toy that can be stuffed with treats, such as cream cheese or peanut butter.

Switch it up – Dogs can become bored with a certain treat. For impromptu training, have a grab bag of a mix of different treats to keep your Shorkie motivated. Try cutting up jerky treats into small pieces and add soft and hard treats to the grab bag; this will keep him intrigued enough to keep learning the new command.

Basic Commands

Teaching your dog, the following basic commands is a rewarding experience for the two of you, and it will strengthen the bonds of friendship. It is important to start teaching your dog while he is still a puppy in order to lay a strong foundation, which will help him grow into a well-behaved dog.

If you have adopted an older dog, you can still teach him these basic commands (if he does not know them already). You simply will need to be more patient and spend extra time reinforcing the new behavior. Training a dog, no matter his age, is a great way to spend time together and to have fun!

Shorkies are fast learners. With your kind and gentle guidance, you will be able to teach your dog how to sit, come, stay etc. in a matter of a few weeks.

Keep in mind while training your Shorkie:

- Keep training sessions short and sweet. Dogs have a short attention span, so opt for several five-minutes classes a day as opposed to one long class.
- Only train your dog when you are in a positive mood. If you are grumpy or irritable, your dog will be able to pick up on your negative vibe.
- Always end each training session by doing a command or trick you know he can do quickly and easily.
- Start off training in an area with no distractions. Once your dog has mastered the commands, try training in a new environment with more distractions.
- Training should always be based on using positive reinforcements, such as treats, toys, playtime and praise. Never, ever yell or physically hurt your dog!

All of the following commands can be done by using a clicker for training. Simply press the clicker whenever you say the command and follow with a treat immediately after.

If you want your dog to sit, do not say "Sit Down Here." Instead, simplify it by saying, "Sit," and reward him immediately. Avoid complicated commands your dog will never understand. Once you choose a command word, do not change it as that will only confuse your puppy.

When training your Shorkie, pay close attention to the tone of your voice. Never yell at your dog as he has very good ears and can hear you very well. A loud, angry voice is not going to teach him anything except the fact that you are upset. Patiently show your dog what you expect of him, speak in a soft, kind voice and praise him affectionally.

CHAPTER 8 Basic Commands

Photo Courtesy of Alita Mercado

Sit

Photo Courtesy of Monique Howard

Teaching your Shorkie to sit is one of the easiest commands.

1. Start with holding a treat near your Shorkie's nose.
2. Move your hand upwards, which will cause his head to follow the snack and lower his bottom to the ground.
3. When he is in a sitting position, say the command, Sit, and give him a reward and praise him.

Be sure to repeat this process a few times daily or until he has mastered it. Ask your Shorkie to sit before mealtime, while going on a walk or any other situations where you need to calm him down.

Stay

Once he has mastered the Sit command, then he is ready for something a little more challenging.

1. Tell your pup, Sit.
2. Open up the palm of your hand. Say, Stay.
3. Start taking a few steps back. If he stays where he is sitting, give him a treat and some praise.
4. Repeat the above; however, each time gradually step further back each time, and if he stays, give him a treat.
5. Always give your Shorkie a reward for staying, even if it was only for a few seconds.
6. Repeat a few times each day until he has mastered the Stay command and can stay at least a minute.

This training command teaches your dog self-control. Don't be discouraged if it takes a little longer to learn.

Down

This is one of the more difficult commands for your dog to master because in order to perform, he needs to get into a submissive posture. While teaching this command, keep the sessions upbeat, fun and relaxed.

1. Choose one of your Shorkie's favorite treats that he can smell and hold inside of your fist but out of sight.
2. Place your fist in front of his nose. When he can smell the treat inside your fist, move your hand slowly toward the ground. His head should follow.
3. Once you reach the ground, slide your hand in front of him, which should encourage his body to lower to the ground along with his head.
4. Once he is in the Down position say, Down, and give him the treat and praise him.

Repeat this command every day until your Shorkie has mastered it. If he tries to lunge forward and grab the treat, say a firm, No, and hide your hand behind your back. Never try pushing him into a lie down position; simply encourage him to lie down on his own by moving your hand towards the ground. Encourage your pup along the way..., he is trying his hardest to please you!

Come

This command can keep your Shorkie out of trouble by helping him return to you if you accidently left the front door open or if you lost your grip on his leash.

1. Place his collar and leash on your pup.
2. Get down to his level and say, Come, while gently tugging on the leash.
3. When he comes to you, reward him with loads of affection and a reward.

Once he has mastered this command using the leash, practice it without the leash but in an enclosed area.

Off

Off can easily become confused with Down. The Off command is used to teach your Shorkie not to jump on people or to climb on certain furniture. The goal is for your dog to keep all four paws on the ground.

1. When your dog jumps up, say a firm, Off, and point to the floor. Once he is standing with all four paws are on the ground, reward his good behavior.
2. If you found your Shorkie on the couch, and he is not allowed to be there, say a firm, Off, and encourage him to come to you. When he comes, reward him with a treat and praise.

Another way to avoid this bad behavior is by simply ignoring it. When he jumps up on you, turn around and act like you are leaving. Wait a few seconds and then try again. Reward your dog when he does not jump up on you.

Leave It

This command will keep your Shorkie safe when curiosity gets the best of him. The purpose of this command is to teach him he is going to get something even yummier if he drops whatever he has in his mouth at your command.

1. Place a reward in both of your hands.
2. Open one of the fists and show him the treat and say, Leave It.
3. Close your fist again, let him sniff, paw or even bark at your fist to try and get it.
4. Once he stops trying, give him the reward that was in your other hand.
5. Repeat this command until he backs away from your hand when you say, Leave It.
6. Once he has mastered the first part of the command, only give him the treat in the second hand when he backs away from you and looks up to you for guidance.

It is very important to keep eye contact with your pup when you are speaking this command. In the second hand, make sure you have a soft and stinky treat and in the other hand, just a normal piece of kibble.

How to introduce the Leash and Collar

Some dogs are quick to embrace their collar and leash, while others seem to shy away from them.

Whether you live in an urban or a rural setting, sooner than later you are going to have to introduce your dog to a collar and a leash. Often the breeder will introduce your Shorkie to a collar when he is only a few weeks old. Do not worry if they did not do this.

The following steps will help you train your pup to use a collar and a leash:

1. Go to a neutral space, such as your living room or backyard, and let him sniff the collar. Put the collar on him when he is distracted and will not even notice you put it on him.
2. The collar should be snug but not so tight it irritates your Shorkie. Once it is around his neck, reward him and praise him. Continue interacting with him to distract him from the fact he is wearing the collar. He might stop occasionally to scratch at it.

CHAPTER 8 Basic Commands

3. If he does not stop obsessing about the collar, remove it and try again later.
4. Put it on again right before his mealtime. Your dog will start to associate the collar with food and will begin to tolerate it. If he scratches at the collar, distract him with a play toy until he forgets about the irritation.

Photo Courtesy of Yvonne McAvoy

**HELPFUL TIP
Short Attention Spans**

Shorkies are adorable and good-natured, but they often have short attention spans, which can make training slightly more difficult. Because of this, you'll need to have patience while training your Shorkie. Avoid negative reinforcement and focus on praise and positive reinforcement. Shorkies are eager to please!

Most dogs love their leash, but there are a few that react like a fish stuck on a hook! They wiggle and squirm as they try to escape. If your dog acts like this, try attaching the leash and letting him run around the yard dragging it behind him. Be sure to supervise your pooch in case he gets tangled up.

Once he looks comfortable with the leash dragging behind him, pick it up and call him to come to you. Give him a reward and praise when he comes. Try holding the leash in your hand and walking with him beside you. You might need to persuade him with treats and encouragement, but once your dog associates the leash with playtime and walks, he will love it.

Take your time and be patient! Eventually, your dog will master walking on the leash in orderly fashion.

Advanced Commands

Basic commands lay the foundation for teaching your Shorkie more advanced commands. So, before you begin with more advanced commands, make sure he has mastered the basic commands above. Otherwise, he will become frustrated and may stop wanting to learn new tricks.

Look

Teach your Shorkie to pay attention to you.

1. Hold a treat between your thumb and pointer finger, so your dog can easily see it.
2. Bring the treat up towards the tip of your nose and hold it there.
3. Give your dog the command, "Look."
4. Hold for a few seconds then praise him and give him the treat.
5. Repeat until he masters the command. Only give him the treat if he is looking directly at you and the treat.

This command lays the groundwork for many different commands, such as fetch or drop it.

No

This might not seem like an advanced command, but dogs tend to quickly ignore the "No" command because they hear it said so often. You will constantly need to reinforce this simple yet important command.

1. Give your Shorkie the Sit command.
2. Take one of his favorite treats out of your pocket and place it on the floor where he can still see it but cannot reach it.
3. When he lunges forward to eat the treat say, "No." Raise your hand in a stop sign. Use your hand as a barrier between him and the treat. Do not yell or hit your dog.
4. You need to be patient with this command as he will try to sneak in a few treats if you become distracted.
5. The goal of this command is for your Shorkie to look at you when you say, "No," and not at the treat. He should then look to you for permission to eat the treat.
6. When he looks at you, pick up the treat and give it to him.
7. Repeat this command until he has mastered it and can wait a minute or two before being allowed to eat the reward.

This command will teach your Shorkie to stop whatever he is doing when he hears the No command.

Roll Over

This is a difficult command to teach because it is physically difficult to guide your dog though the movements without having to help him roll over.

1. Tell your dog to go into the Down position.
2. Hold a treat between your thumb and pointing finger, so he can easily see it. Place it close to his nose.
3. Do a backwards circle with the treat in front of his gaze, causing him to follow the treat. The movement should result in him flopping over on his side while trying to roll over.
4. The first few times you practice this, might have to help your Shorkie roll over, so he can follow the treat. Say command, Roll Over, as he is in the process of rolling and give him the reward at the end.

CHAPTER 9
Traveling

Taking your Shorkie on a journey is fun for everyone. After all, a vacation is not the same if the whole family is not there! Whether you are off to see relatives or to the beach, your dog will love exploring his new surroundings with you by his side. However, traveling with your dog means planning in advance, so everything goes smoothly and stress free.

Photo Courtesy of Scott & Karen Evans

CHAPTER 9 Traveling

Preparing Your Shorkie for Travel

If you are planning on traveling with your furry friend for the first time, there are a few things you can do beforehand to make the trip less stressful for you and your Shorkie. Here is everything you need to pack to make sure your trip is as successful as possible:

FUN FACT
Popularity

According to the dog comparison website dogell.com, Shorkies are the 597th most popular dog breed. Because Shorkies are such a new breed, it's difficult to use this statistic to determine how desirable this breed is. It's likely that their popularity will continue to grow as more people learn about the joys of owning a Shorkie.

- **Food:** Pack enough food for the duration of the trip as switching your dog's food can cause him to have an upset tummy. If you are traveling for a long period of time, research whether your dog's food is available at your final destination.

- **Water:** Throw in a water bottle or two to keep your pup hydrated during the duration of the trip. Do not allow your Shorkie to drink water from an unfamiliar source, such as a creek or puddle.

- **Food and water dishes:** Place your dog's food and water dishes somewhere you can easily access them throughout the trip. If you are tight on space, invest in a set of pop-up dishes.

- **Crate or carrier:** Depending on your method of traveling, you will need either a hard cover crate or a soft cover carrier. Make sure you find a carrying case that is comfortable for your Shorkie as it will most likely be used as his bedroom when you reach your final destination. How to choose an appropriate crate is discussed in the following pages.

- **Toys:** Do not forget to throw in some of your pup's all-time, favorite toys for the journey. This will keep him distracted and help relieve stress.

- **Blankets and doggy beds:** A blanket for the inside of his crate will help keep your Shorkie warm and will have a familiar scent, which will calm him down. Bring your dog's doggy bed along if possible.

- **Collar, leash, harness and ID tags:** Be sure to place your dog's collar and ID tags on him before leaving the house and do not remove them until you return home. This is in case you accidently get separated from your Shorkie.

Photo Courtesy of Ashley Barron

- **Supplies:** Traveling with a dog can get messy. To be fully prepared, bring along potty pads, baby wipes, baggies, paper towels and a pet-friendly stain remover.

- **Medications:** If your Shorkie is taking any type of medicine or supplements, make sure you have enough for the duration of your vacation.

- **Health and vaccinations certificates:** Always take your Shorkie's medical information with you while traveling. It will provide proof he is vaccinated and will provide the vet with needed information if there is an emergency.

CHAPTER 9 Traveling

Traveling by Car

Whether you are taking a short or long journey, you will want to make the trip enjoyable for your Shorkie.

It might be tempting to let your dog sit in the front seat or to move about freely in the backseat, but if you are in an accident that was caused by a distraction from your dog, you could be found accountable. Even worse, you or your dog or other parties might be injured.

Do...
- Secure your Shorkie inside of a hard-cover crate that is harnessed in with a seatbelt or is placed on the floor.
- Bring along plenty of water to keep your puppy hydrated, even more so during the hot summer months.
- If you have the air conditioner on or the window open, make sure it is not blowing directly on your Shorkie. Also, if the window is open, make sure your dog cannot access it and accidently jump out.
- Take regular bathroom breaks, not only for your dog to go potty, but also to stretch his legs and to rehydrate.

Photo Courtesy of Debra Rosenblatt

- Bring along familiar items to help your Shorkie feel relaxed throughout the trip.
- If your dog suffers from motion sickness, ask your vet to prescribe a travel medication and follow the vet's instructions.

Don't…
- Do not allow your dog to sit in the front seat or travel with his head hanging out of an open window.
- Do not feed your Shorkie at least two hours prior to traveling in order to prevent motion sickness.
- Never leave your dog inside of a hot car - it only takes a few minutes for your Shorkie to become overheated - which could be fatal.

Photo Courtesy of Sandra Cadieux

If your dog is wary of the car, let him explore the vehicle while it is turned off. Then, turn the car on, so he can get accustomed to the sound of the motor while he is inside. Praise your dog and reward his good behavior. Place him in his crate and take him for a short drive around the neighborhood with someone sitting in the backseat next to his crate. Make sure the final destination is somewhere fun, such as the park, beach or playing fetch in the yard.

> **FUN FACT**
> **Attempted Theft**
>
> Benny the Shorkie rose to a small level of fame when he was kidnapped in the summer of 2019 by a Manhattan dog walker employed by a dog-walking app. The dog walker had hoped to gift the adorable pooch to one of his friends, but thanks to the diligent work of the NYPD, Benny was reunited with his parents shortly after his abduction.

The Right Crate for Long Distance Car Travel:

When taking your dog for long car trips you want to ensure he is safe and comfortable. Not having your Shorkie inside of his crate is not only dangerous for you but also for your pooch.

Size – Dog crates were not created as one-size fits all. If you try and squish your pup into a carrier that is too small, you are going to end up with a very unhappy dog, which will also result in a stubborn dog that refuses to re-enter his crate once released.

Purchase a crate that is designed for your dog's breed and weight. When in doubt, it always is preferable to go bigger instead of smaller. Do remember though, a bigger crate means your dog will have more space to move around, but this also means he may involuntarily slide around in the crate with the car's natural motion. So, choose your crate size carefully.

Soft vs. hard-cover – As noted earlier, a soft carrier might be more comfortable for your Shorkie. However, for car travel, a hard-cover crate is preferable as it will provide your dog with more protection if you get into an accident. Another advantage is hard-cover crates are easier to clean if your dog gets carsick or has an accident.

Harness – Many car crates come with a built-in option to be fastened to the seatbelt for extra stability. You can also purchase a separate harness designed to fasten your dog crate to the backseat or seatbelt. By fastening the crate, you create a more secure ride for your dog as the crate will not slide around on sharp corners or fly around if you come to a sudden stop.

Visibility – Shorkies are very curious and enjoy observing their surroundings. Look for a crate that provides an unhindered view and lots of fresh air. If your Shorkie is nervous inside of the car, the more visibility, the better.

Traveling by Plane

Flying with a dog is stressful, but there are a few things that help relieve the stress. With some extra planning and security precautions, your Shorkie will be a seasoned traveler in no time!

Feed your dog four hours before the actual flight to make sure he has relieved himself and is well exercised and comfortable inside of his crate when you leave. This will lessen your Shorkie's stress level. Withholding food two to four hours before traveling will also reduce travel sickness.

Here is everything you need to know to help your pooch become a frequent flyer.

Snub-nosed dog

Shorkie are considered to be a brachycephalic breed, meaning they have short snouts. Snub-nose dogs, such as Bull Dogs, Boston Terriers, Pugs and Shih Tzu can suffer from respiratory issues while traveling by air. Also, they take longer to cool off when they become overheated. Shorkies have inherited their snub-nose from one of their parents – the Shih Tzu.

No airline will allow snub-nose dogs to travel as cargo because the extreme changes in temperature and air quality make them very vulnerable

Photo Courtesy of Rebecca Mullan

CHAPTER 9   Traveling

to stress and overheating. The good news is many airlines will let you travel with your Shorkie in the main cabin for a small fee.

Research, research and research – Before purchasing your tickets, investigate which airlines are pet-friendly that travel to your destination. A few airlines refuse to accept any type of brachycephalic dog or cat on their flights. Yet, there are several pet-friendly airlines who will happily transport your snub-nose dog.

Once you have found an airline that will transport your Shorkie in the main cabin, you will need to phone before purchasing your ticket for the following reasons:

- Most airlines limit the number of dogs per flight. Ask if there is availability for the dates you plan to travel for transporting your Shorkie. Also, inquire about any extra costs and if any special paperwork is required.
- The specified kennel dimensions to fit under the seat in front of you differ for each airline. Just because the crate you plan to purchase says "airline approved" does not necessarily mean it is suitable to be used on all aircrafts.

When purchasing your ticket, make sure to find the most direct flight. The less stops the better. Rates for traveling with your Shorkie in the main cabin can vary from $70 to $400 depending on the airline and the distance.

Many airlines do not require pet owners to provide health records for their pets, others some will request a copy of your dog's health and vaccination records at least seventy-two hours before the flight. Some airlines will require you to sign a behavior agreement, stating that your Shorkie will behave for the duration of the flight. If you are traveling internationally, be sure to check with the airline for any special requirements.

Ask your vet for advice –If your pooch is overweight, the vet can formulate a weight loss plan to help him lose those extra pounds before the journey. This is especially important because obese, snub-nose dogs are at an even higher risk while traveling as their airways can collapse.

Choose the right crate – Yes, we're back to crates, and there's a reason. Whereas a hard-side crate is often best for car travel, the best type of crate for traveling via plane is a soft-sided carrier as it can easily fit under the seat in front of you. Hard-cover crates are quite cumbersome to fit under the seat and are heavier to carry around inside the airport.

When choosing a crate for air travel, look for one that is slightly larger than necessary to give your Shorkie a little extra breathing room and space to stretch out. If you are taking your Shorkie cross-country or overseas, opt for a carrier that expands to give him a little extra space. Many carriers or crates come with an attachable water dispenser, which is essential for keeping your dog well-hydrated during the flight.

In case of an accident, place a disposable potty pad on the bottom of the crate. Plus, it will be handy to bring along gallon size Ziplock bags in case your Shorkie goes potty during the flight. You can easily clean up and dispose of the soiled pads.

A WORD OF CAUTION: Your doggy crate will count as a piece of your allotted carry-ons so be sure to pack accordingly.

Once inside the airplane, your Shorkie has to stay inside of his carrier for the duration of the flight. You are not permitted to take him out of his carrier to cuddle with him or to place the carrier on the seat beside you.

Hydrate, Hydrate, Hydrate - Hydration is essential for making the airplane journey safer for your pooch. Before traveling, get your Shorkie used to drinking water from the carrier case.

If your dog is hesitant to drink from the water bottle, then entice him by filling it with lukewarm chicken broth. Water dispensers have a ball inside of the cap that rolls around when touched, releasing water. You might have to encourage your Shorkie by rolling the ball around and releasing the irresistible scent of chicken broth. Reward him when he drinks from the water bottle, and slowly wean him off the chicken broth by replacing it with water.

Treats – Just as babies cannot pop their ears during the change of pressurization upon take-off and landing, your Shorkie can't either. To avoid this, give your pup a few pieces of a jerky treat to chew on to avoid any ear issues during the flight. Be careful not to give him too much as he could get air sick.

Photo Courtesy of Carrie Moore

CHAPTER 9   Traveling

Lodging Away from Home

Figuring out how to travel with a dog takes a little extra planning to find a pet-friendly hotel or vacation rental. Here are some helpful hints to take the inconvenience out of traveling with your Shorkie.

Talk directly to the hotel – When traveling with your dog, phone the hotel directly and ask about their fees and policies. Here are some practical questions to ask:

- Does the hotel charge a fee per night or a flat fee for the entire duration of your Shorkie's stay?
- Are there restrictions on the type of dog breed, size or weight?
- Is the entire hotel pet-friendly or are there only designated floors and areas for dogs?
- Are you allowed to leave your dog alone in the room unsupervised?
- Will you need to make a damage deposit?
- Are there puppy-sitters or dog-walkers to hire?

Consider your dog's behavior – Nobody knows your Shorkie better than you. If your dog tends to get nervous in elevators, then ask for a room at floor level, or if he tends to bark at people who walk past the window, request a room on a higher floor. Leave the television on when you leave the room, so he will not be able to hear strange noises outside of the room and get nervous.

Have a back-up plan – If the hotel staff inform you cannot leave your pooch alone in the room, hire a dog-walker or puppy-sitter. Another option is to take your Shorkie to the groomer or a doggy day-spa, if necessary.

If you are allowed to leave your dog alone, always give the hotel staff a heads up that you are going out and leave your cell number in case of any noise complaints. Make sure your pup has become acclimated to his new surroundings before you leave the room. Be sure to place the "Do Not Disturb" sign on the door before leaving. Place your Shorkie inside of his crate with the door shut. Avoid leaving your dog unattended for long periods.

Discover pet-friendly restaurants – Most hotels will have a list of pet-friendly restaurants nearby, and often if the hotel is pet-friendly, it will allow pets inside of their onsite restaurant or lobby bar. Most restaurants with outside seating welcome dogs as long they are on a leash and are behaving.

Follow a routine – Dogs love routine. It is essential you stick to your Shorkie's regular schedule while traveling. Feed and exercise your dog at the same time as you would at home. When you first go into the hotel room, set-up his potty pads and show him where to go the bathroom.

Research the area for dog-friendly activities – After all, it is not simply your holiday but it is also your dog's holiday! Research the area for activities your Shorkie will enjoy, such as hiking, exploring breweries, fresh markets, monuments or parks. A bonus of keeping him busy during the day is he will sleep better at night.

When staying with family or friends:
- Staying with family and friends for the holidays is already a challenge. Adding your dog to the mix simply makes things more interesting. No matter where you are staying, your Shorkie needs to practice proper pet-etiquette to be the perfect house guest.
- Never assume your Shorkie is welcomed to stay over as a house guest. Even if he has stayed over at someone's house before, always ask the host if your dog is welcomed to stay again. Having house guests can be very stressful, and adding a dog into the mix of things can add more stress for the host.
- Another factor to take into consideration is the host or other house guests might have allergies to dogs, or there might be small children that are uncomfortable around dogs.
- Ask your host where would be an appropriate area for your dog to go to the bathroom. Do not assume your pooch is allowed on the furniture or a free-run of the house. If things do not work out as planned, have a contingency plan, such as a pet-friendly hotel or a reputable boarding kennel.

Kenneling vs. Dog-sitters

As much as it breaks your heart, there are occasions you will need to travel without your Shorkie. The hard part is deciding whether to board your pup in a kennel or to hire a dog-sitter while you are out of town. There is no perfect answer, but taking into consideration your dog's age, temperament and needs will make the decision a little easier.

Boarding Kennels

Boarding kennels are basically a pet hotel for your dog.

Your Shorkie's stay at the boarding kennel includes grooming, attention and exercise. Depending on the kennel you choose, they will offer a variety of packages and prices to cater to your dog's individual requirements. If you are considering this option, here are some of the benefits and some of the drawbacks:

CHAPTER 9 Traveling

Advantages to kennels:

- While you are away, kennels provide a secure environment for your dog and include a trained staff who constantly monitor the pets to help prevent any incidents.
- Boarding kennels host other friendly pets, giving your Shorkie plenty of fun opportunities to socialize with other dogs and people.
- Your dog will follow a strict schedule during his stay, which will reduce his stress levels. From your pup's first day there, he will be fed and exercised according to his schedule.
- Often there is a veterinarian onsite or on-call if there are any emergencies. This option is especially helpful, if your Shorkie has chronic health issues, as he will receive constant monitoring.

Disadvantages to a kennel:

- With all the different pets staying at the kennel, things can get quite chaotic and noisy at times, which can be stressful for anxious or sensitive

Photo Courtesy of Yanet Duran

- dogs. If your Shorkie tends to get stressed out in new environments or around other animals, boarding your dog might not be the best option.
- Although the kennel staff do their best to keep circumstances in check, certain situations can get out of control. There is a certain risk factor of injury if your Shorkie accidently gets into a scuffle with another dog.
- Depending on the size of the kennel, staff could mix up food, toys or blankets between different pets. Often, this does not cause too many problems, except perhaps an upset tummy.

All boarding kennels require their pet guests have up-to-date vaccines. Puppies and dogs are required to have received their Rabies and Bordetella (Kennel Cough) vaccine at least seven days prior to their planned arrival. Bordetella is an airborne upper-respiratory infection. There are more than fifty-seven different strains, and the current vaccine only protects against fourteen.

Currently, there is no way to fully protect your dog from kennel cough as it is very contagious. For this very reason, it is extremely important to search for a boarding kennel that daily sanitizes everything your dog might come into contact with, such as playground areas, daycare areas, toys, food and water dishes, etc.

Kennels have the right to refuse admittance to any dog if the pet owner lacks adequate proof of their dog's vaccinations, the dog has a serious health condition or displays aggressive behavior.

Dog-sitter

A dog-sitter is someone who will care for your dog by either dropping by your house a few times each day or by staying overnight in your house for the duration of your time away. Having a dog-sitter stay overnight is the ideal solution if your pup suffers from separation anxiety or if you prefer not to leave him alone at night.

Advantages to a dog-sitter:
- While you are away, your Shorkie is in the comfort of his own home. No need to worry about your pooch being exposed to a new environment, people or other animals.
- The risk of accidents or injury is reduced because a single person is devoted to caring for your Shorkie.
- Your dog-sitter will carefully follow all of your care instructions for your dog and perhaps even water your plants, if you ask them to. If you have a younger pup, you can teach the dog-sitter how to work on your dog's obedience training and basic commands.

- A dog-sitter will directly communicate with you if there are any problems, etc. The direct line of communication will give you peace of mind, so you can focus on your holiday.

Disadvantages to a dog-sitter:
- A dog-sitter needs to come into your house and it is imperative you and your Shorkie trust her or him. If your pooch is protective of his home or does not react well to new people, perhaps a dog-sitter is not the best option.
- Having a dog-sitter stay inside of your home requires extra preparation, such as preparing the guest bedroom in which they will stay.
- During holiday season, it can be almost impossible to find a reliable dog-sitter. Be sure to book ahead of time.
- If you hired a dog-sitter to drop by a few times a day and it snows, they might not be able to get to your house regularly.

Finding a professional and responsible individual to take care of your Shorkie while you are away is a big decision that should not be taken lightly. Here are a few suggestions to help you find a reputable dog-sitter to care for your dog:

- **Ask your veterinarian** – If you have an older dog with health issues, finding a dog-sitter with a good rapport with your vet will give you peace of mind, if there is a medical emergency.

- **Word of mouth** – Anyone can look good on paper, but a qualified, reputable dog-sitter often will be recommended by friends or family.

- **Ask for references** – A reputable dog-sitter should have a list of previous and regular clients who would be willing to verify their professionalism.

- **Look for a certified dog-sitter** – There are two nationwide agencies that trains and certifies dog-sitters: Pet Sitters International (PSI) and The National Association of Professional Pet Sitters (NAPPS). Check out their webpages to locate a certified dog-sitter in your area, plus see their reviews from previous clients.

You will have to consider your Shorkie's personality and needs to make the best choice while you are out of town. Carefully consider the advantages and drawbacks of each option and weigh them against your pup's requirements in order to make the ideal decision. If you cannot decide which is the best choice, you can always try a short stay at the kennel and another with the dog-sitter before your trip to see how your dog reacts.

CHAPTER 10
Nutrition

How much should you feed your Shorkie? Does the food you have chosen for your dog meet his nutritional requirements? What are the nutritional requirements for your dog?

Photo Courtesy of Anastasia Berglind

Importance of a Wholesome Diet

As a responsible doggy parent, you will want to give your Shorkie the best, including the foods you choose to feed him. Just like humans, dogs require essential nutrients to develop properly and to be healthy. Why is it important to feed your dog a high-quality diet?

The quality of food you choose to feed your dog directly affects his present and his long-term health. The old saying, "You are what you eat." applies to your dog as much as yourself. Foods made with high-quality ingredients mean a better-quality of life, which results in fewer skin conditions, ear infections, digestive issues and the list goes on and on. The impact of good nutrition does not end there as your dog's diet can affect his behavior as well.

Here is how the quality or quantity of food your dog eats affects his overall health, mood and personality.

Unbalanced diet – An unbalanced diet can cause your Shorkie to have urinary tract infections that cause him to become unusually irritable and stressed out because of pain and discomfort. A well-balanced, high-quality dog food will ensure your dog maintains ideal health.

Lack of food – If your pup is not receiving enough food throughout the day, he will feel hungry and may even resort to destructive behaviors, such as scavenging or eating his feces. Dogs that are receiving inadequate nutrients in their daily diet develop a condition called "pica" which causes them to eat non-food items, such as dirt and plants.

Quality of pet food ingredients – It is important your Shorkie receives the right type of food for his breed and age. For example, a puppy food will contain higher levels of the fatty acid DHA, which increases their mental alertness. On the other hand, senior dog food is enriched with antioxidants, which feeds their brain and help them learn more complicated tasks. Also, studies have shown older dogs that have always received a wholesome dog food suffer from fewer behavior changes common with cognitive decline.

Choosing to feed your Shorkie a well-balanced diet will promote stable blood sugar levels throughout the day instead of glucose ups and downs. This affects your pup's serotonin levels. Serotonin is considered to be the happy hormone, which will improve your dog's concentration, behavior and his training response. Another advantage to good nutrition is it will keep your Shorkie's immune system and metabolism functioning properly.

There is no brand of dog food that is suitable for all types of dogs. A dog's age, breed, size, medical history, immune system and lifestyle all need to be considered when choosing a wholesome dog food. Talk to your veterinarian about suggestions on what type of dog foods are suitable for your Shorkie's optimal health.

When a dog gets sick, we assume it is due to exposure to something external, and we never think it could be what we are feeding him.

Here are some common health issues that are directly related your dog's diet:

- **Heart disease** – Recent studies by the FDA have discovered grain-free dog foods are directly related to Canine Dilated Cardiomyopathy (CDC), which causes the dog's heart to enlarge and prevents the blood to circulate freely throughout the body. The FDA is recommending pet owners to avoid grain-free food. Dogs need a diet based on high-quality proteins, natural fats, vegetables and whole grains to meet their dietary needs to combat heart disease.
- **Diabetes** – Overweight dogs often develop diabetes. There is no cure for diabetes. A dog with diabetes will require daily insulin shots and extra medical attention. The best prevention is to keep your Shorkie on a healthy diet and to give him an active lifestyle. Avoid dog foods that contain starchy fillers and sugar, which offer little to no nutritional value and will only spike your dog's blood sugar levels.
- **Food allergies** – Food allergies can cause your dog to have hives, itchy skin, digestive issues and a swollen face. Allergens can include things like chicken, dairy products and corn.
- **Obesity** – Your Shorkie does not need too many calories each day, so be sure to follow the instructions on the bag of food for his weight, age and breed. Obesity can cause breathing issues, joint pain and shorten your dog's lifespan.

Human Foods to Avoid

Slipping your Shorkie a treat or two from the table can be tempting, but it can cause your dog some serious health problems, or it can even be fatal. You might be surprised at some of the food your pup needs to avoid... at all costs!

Xylitol – Xylitol is a common sweetener used in baked goods, toothpaste and diet products. It causes your dog's blood sugar to drop and leads to liver failure.

Avocado – Dogs are allergic to persin, which is found in avocados. Persin is not just found in the flesh of the fruit but is also in the leaves, peel, seed, bark, etc. If you have an avocado tree in your backyard, keep your dog away from it.

Alcohol – A little bit of beer, wine or liquor can be fatal for a dog the size of your Shorkie. It causes coordination problems, vomiting, diarrhea, breathing issues, coma and finally death.

CHAPTER 10 Nutrition

Garlic and Onions – Keep all types of garlic and onions away from your pooch – fresh, dry, powdered, dehydrated or cooked. Even the tiniest amount can cause your dog's blood count to drop, making him anemic.

Any type of caffeine – All types of caffeine are fatal for your Shorkie, including tea, cocoa, energy drinks, soda and coffee. If you think your dog accidently consumed a product with caffeine, get your dog to your veterinarian as soon as possible.

Grapes or raisins – Grapes and raisins might seem like the perfect sized treat for your dog, but a few can cause kidney failure. If you think your Shorkie might have eaten some grapes, watch out for severe vomiting and sluggish behavior.

Dairy products – Avoid the temptation of sharing your ice cream cone with your Shorkie on a hot summer day. Dairy products can cause your dog to experience digestive discomfort and diarrhea. Many dogs are allergic to dairy products, often causing itchy skin.

Macadamia nuts – Only six macadamia nuts can make your pooch seriously ill. Eating chocolate with macadamia nuts intensifies the symptoms, even leading to death. Macadamia nuts can cause vomiting, muscle shakes, fever and loss of muscle control.

Chocolate – All types of chocolate, including white chocolate, are deadly for dogs. Even the smallest piece can cause your Shorkie to vomit and to have diarrhea. It can cause heart issues, seizures, tremors and even be fatal.

Bones or fat trimmings – Even though it might seem second nature to give your dog a bone, smaller dogs, like Shorkies, can easily choke on them, or the bone can splinter off and cut up the inside of your pup's digestive system. Pieces of fat or grease can cause your Shorkie to devolp pancreatitis.

Pitted fruits – Fruits such as peaches, persimmons, cherries and plums have pits or seeds that can get lodged in your dog's intestines causing a blockage. Some pits, such as from a plum or a peach, contain cyanide, which is fatal.

Raw eggs – Raw eggs are a source of bacteria, such as Salmonella or E. coli. Avoid feeding your Shorkie any type of raw animal products - fish, beef or chicken.

Salt – Eating too much salt can cause sodium ion poisoning, vomiting, diarrhea, fever and seizures, and it can even

HELPFUL TIP
Which Food?

You may be wondering whether it's better to feed your Shorkie wet or dry food. Due to Shorkies' predisposition for dental issues, it's recommended to feed them dry kibble instead of wet food. Be sure to choose a kibble that is made for small dogs.

be fatal if left untreated. Moral of the story: Do not share your pretzels or salted popcorn with your pooch!

Raw yeast dough – Before baking, raw yeast dough needs to rise. When consumed by your dog the dough will swell up inside of his stomach. The dough can grow to the point where it stretches out your dog's abdomen causing extreme pain. The yeast can also cause alcohol poisoning.

If your Shorkie got into the pantry and ate something he shouldn't have, call your local vet immediately or call the Animal Poison Control Center (ASPCA) – (888) 426-4435.

There are some human foods that are suitable for dogs to eat in moderation. If you decide to give your pup an occasional treat from your table, make sure it is not seasoned, fatty or raw.

Here are few ideas regarding what is suitable:

- Lean meats that are well-cooked. Be sure to remove any excess fat, skin or bones that he could choke on.
- Certain fresh fruits, such as thin slices of apples, bananas or watermelon all make yummy treats for your Shorkie. Be sure to remove any seeds, peel or stem that could get stuck in your dog's digestive track.
- Some vegetables, such as carrot sticks, green beans or a slice of cucumber, make a great snack. Never let your Shorkie eat any type of raw potatoes.
- Cooked, plain white rice or noodles with a piece of boiled chicken breast might be the solution if your pup has an upset tummy.

Commercial Dog Food

The dog food market is saturated with products all claiming to be "wholesome, complete and balanced."

Commercial dog food has improved in leaps and bounds in the last few years. In the past, there were only a few generic brands on the shelf. Today, there are all types of options to choose from, which cater to different breeds, ages and diets. However, there are so many choices these days that choosing which type of dog food is best for your Shorkie can be quite overwhelming. In this section, we will discuss everything you need to know about commercially prepared dog foods.

There are two basic types of commercially prepared dog food: canned foods and dry kibble. Commercially produced fresh dog food gets an honorable mention because it is just starting to emerge.

CHAPTER 10 Nutrition

Canned foods – Canned foods consist of 35% to 75% water depending on the quality and are mixed with a variety of meats, such as beef, salmon, chicken or venison. Canned food is also referred to as wet food and comes in small tins, trays, pouches or rolls. It is packaged using an extremely high heat-sterilization method, which destroys some of the essential nutrients and vitamins. The sterilization and vacuum sealing process ensure a longer shelf-life without the need of using harmful preservatives.

All dogs love canned foods because they are packed with flavor. However, because of the processing method, they are nutritionally deficient. If you want your pooch to get all of his daily nutritional requirements, you have to give him a huge portion of canned food at every meal, which will definitely result in weight gain.

Some pet owners try to entice their fussy dogs to eat their meals by mixing a small portion of canned food with dried food. Canned foods are beneficial for dogs who dislike drinking water or have a history of urinary tract issues.

Photo Courtesy of Tammy Szanto

Dry kibble – The majority of dogs in the U.S. are fed dry kibble. Their popularity is due to the convenience of purchasing and of feeding. Generally speaking, dry dog food requires zero preparation and does not have any special storage requirements.

The following is a list of different types of methods used to produce dry kibble:

- **Extrusion:** This is one of the most common methods of manufacturing dog food. All of the ingredients are first ground into a fine powder, then combined together and formed into kibble. The kibble is cooked in a pressure/steam cooker then placed in a convection oven with hot air to remove the excess moisture. Recent studies have shown that the kibble's exposure to extreme temperatures removes the majority of nutrients and vitamins.
- **Baked:** Baking is similar to extrusion but at a lower temperature, so it maintains more nutrients. Baking also uses wheat gluten to bind the ingredients together and artificial preservatives to lengthen the shelf life.
- **Cold-pressed:** A newbie on the dog food aisle but gaining popularity quickly, cold-pressed ingredients are prepared fresh and then ground together and dried before being pressed. They are cooked at a low heat to preserve the vitamins and nutrients.
- **Freeze dried:** This prepared food is placed in a type of vacuum oven that removes any excess moisture. The process preserves the nutrients, making it one of the most natural dry food options. Freeze-dried foods have a long shelf life without the need of harmful preservatives. Some freeze-dried foods might need to be hydrated with water before serving.

Fresh food – The newcomer on the dog food aisle is slowly gaining popularity as a convenient alternative to making your own homemade dog food. Often, fresh dog food is made from the freshest organic ingredients and is served in recyclable serving trays.

One of the main advantages to fresh food is the high-nutritional value due to the low level of processing required. On the other hand, since it does not contain chemical preservatives nor has it been sterilized like standard dog food, fresh dog food doesn't stay fresh very long. Most fresh dog food products have a maximum lifespan of seven to fourteen days maximum and need to be stored in the refrigerator or freezer.

With so many different options and choices of dog food, it is easy to understand why pet owners feel overwhelmed. The different types of food mentioned above each have their own pros and cons; no one type of dog food is the "best" for your Shorkie. The final decision depends on what is best for your budget, time, convenience, personal preferences and ethical values. Most importantly, of course, are your dog's health and his personal preferences.

How to Read Dog Food Labels

One of the keys to giving your Shorkie a healthy life is to make sure he is eating a wholesome diet. Due to the wide variety of different types of dog foods available, it can be almost impossible to decide which kind is best for your pet. On the positive side, if you look past the marketing and packaging of the outside, you will discover what you really need to know by looking at the list of ingredients.

A general rule of thumb: If humans are not allowed to eat it, then you should not feed it to your dog either. The first ingredient listed on the food label comprises the most weight. Continue reading to learn which ingredients to watch out for and why they can be harmful to your Shorkie:

Food to avoid:
- **Rendered foods** – Rendered meat is often listed as rendered chicken, pork or animal by-product meal. Rendered meat is a mix of animal parts, such as brains, blood, spleens, entails and internal organs. Many times, it might include body parts from discarded animals that were considered unfit for human consumption because they were expired or the animal was sick. The nutritional value of rendered meal products is very low and can be a source of salmonella and toxins.

- **Artificial Preservatives** – When choosing a dog food, make sure ethoxyquin, BHA and BHT are not included in the ingredient list. The National Institute of Health has deemed BHA and BHT to be a carcinogenic and unfit for human consumption. Ethoxyquin is directly linked to kidney failure, cancer and chronic immune diseases in both humans and animals.

- **Food Coloring** – Many dog food brands add food coloring to their kibble and treats to make them look more appealing and appetizing. Let's be honest, your dog does not care about the color of his food, just as long as it is tasty. Be aware of food dyes, such as Blue 2, Red 40 or Yellow 5 because they are linked to health issues in humans, such as allergies, hyperactivity and cancer.

- **Propylene Glycol** – Propylene Glycol is a common ingredient in pet food and antifreeze, (which is extremely toxic for dogs). Some dog food manufacturers use this additive to reduce moisture from building up in the packaging, preventing bacterial growth while lengthening the product's shelf-life.

- **Too much corn and rice fillers** – Corn and rice are common fillers in dog foods; however, your Shorkie does not need a carbohydrate-rich diet. A low-protein diet is directly related to obesity in small dogs. Avoid dog food and treats that list corn or rice as one of the first three ingredients. Foods high in corn and rice can also cause chronic digestive issues, such as bloating, gas and diarrhea.
- **Nondescript fats** – Fat is essential for your Shorkie's health. Many dog food products vaguely list "animal fat" as one of the ingredients, which basically is fat derived from sick or rancid animals. Instead, opt for a dog food that actually specifies the type of fat they use, such as "salmon fat" instead of fish fat or "coconut oil" instead of vegetable oil, etc.
- **Sugar** – Many dog foods contain sugar as it can mask a bitter flavor and improve the texture of the kibble. More importantly, dog manufacturers add sugar to cause your dog to become addicted to their brand of food. Once a dog is addicted to sugar, it is very difficult to convince him to eat a healthier, sugar-free option. Additive sugars that should be avoided are: cane sugar, beet pulp, corn syrup, sucrose, fructose-glucose, xylitol, molasses and sorbitol.
- **MSG** – Monosodium glutamate (MSG) is a well-known flavor enhancer for Chinese food and dog food. MSG over-stimulates your brain, which causes your body to produce a hormone called dopamine and to make food almost seem addictive. Recent studies have shown MSG when consumed regularly by dogs, can cause serious brain damage, obesity and behavioral issues, etc.

Foods to look for:

Finding a wholesome dog food can be a challenge, but it is not impossible. A wholesome dog food will include a variety of ingredients, such as meat, veggies, grains and even fruit. Now that we have discussed what types of ingredients to shy away from, here are some good ingredients to look for:

- **Meat** – Your Shorkie needs protein for a healthy body and immune system. Look for commercial dog foods made from real sources of human-grade meat, such as chicken, beef, salmon, rabbit, etc.
- **Whole Meat Meal** – Often meal is confused with by-products such as rendered meats. However, whole meat meal is a high source of protein and is simply another way of saying ground meat. The ingredient list should, specify the type of whole meat meal used, such as chicken, beef, etc. Meat meal is ground up and then dried to a 10% moisture level, making the protein level at least 65% and with approximately 12% to 14% fat. This provides additional nutrients for your dog.

- **Carbohydrates and grains** – Whole grains are an excellent source of energy for your dog and will aid his digestion. Avoid dog foods made from corn, soy or white rice; instead, opt for higher quality ingredients, such as brown rice, whole oats, quinoa, barley and peas. Of course, carbohydrates and grains should never be one of the first ingredients on the ingredient list.
- **Vegetables and fruits** – These provide essential vitamins, antioxidants, fiber and minerals. For example, sweet potatoes are an excellent source of potassium, vitamin B and antioxidants. Cranberries provide vitamin C and prevent urinary tract infections and kill off harmful bacteria that can damage your dog's teeth.
- **Fats** – Fats get a bad rap but they are necessary for your Shorkie's overall health, proper cell function and digestion. Fats help your dog absorb vitamins and minerals and, keep his coat and teeth in tip-top shape.

Photo Courtesy of Van Abad

Look for wholesome fats like Omega-3 fatty acids and Omega-6, canola oils, salmon fat, olive and coconut oils.

An ingredient list does matter:
- Dog food labels that include "flavor," such as chicken or beef flavored. This indicates the food was made with a very small percentage of the real meat and largely contains artificial flavoring.
- The same ingredient is listed multiple times but under a different name, such as sugar, high fructose corn syrup, sucrose, etc.
- The packaging states a food is made "with" a certain protein - manufacturers are only required to use 3% of protein in the dog food.

Even though each brand of dog food claims it provides everything required for your dog's health, it does not mean the food is really healthy. Take the time to carefully read the ingredient list and make a well-informed decision based on the ingredients and not based on the flashy packaging.

Making Homemade Dog Food

A homemade dog food diet is not hard to design, but it does require a certain amount of discipline and planning to prepare. Homemade dog food is not about throwing a bunch of ingredients in the slow-cooker and hoping for the best as it needs to be "complete and well-balanced" by providing all of your Shorkie's nutritional requirements. Always consult your vet before switching your dog to any diet, including a homemade one.

The following guidelines will help you create your own balanced, homemade dog food recipe:

Meat products – Protein should make up 50% to 65% of your Shorkie's diet. Use lean meats without the skin and with the fat cut off. Include in your dog's diet both chicken, fish and red meat without bones. Make sure the meat is cut up into small pieces, so your dog can chew and digest it easily. Use 5% beef liver in your preparation as it is very nutritious.

Eggs – Eggs are an excellent source of protein. Smaller dogs, such as your Shorkie, can eat half of one whole egg per day.

Dairy – Most dogs tolerate plain yogurt, cottage cheese and ricotta cheese. If your dog is lactose intolerant, try using goat milk products instead. Avoid using other types of cheese as they are high in cholesterol and calories.

Starchy vegetables – Potatoes, sweet potatoes and squashes, peas and beans are a great source of fiber and are healthy calories for your dog. If your dog is overweight, you need to limit the amount of starchy vegetables used in your dog food. (Starchy veggies need to be cooked before serving to your dog.)

Other vegetables – Leafy greens are low in calories and jam-packed with wholesome nutrients for your dog. Avoid using raw, cruciferous vegetables, such as cauliflower or broccoli, as they can cause digestive discomfort. Blend and chop the vegetables before adding them to the meat mixture when cooking.

Fruits – Fruits provide fiber to support your dog's digestive health plus other nutrients and antioxidants that contribute to your Shorkie's overall health and longevity. Bananas, apples, berries and papaya are all good options. Avoid grapes and raisins as they can cause kidney failure.

Grains – Use whole grains, such as quinoa, barley, brown rice, whole oats and pasta. However, all grains must be well-cooked so they can be properly digested by your dog. Be aware that cooked white rice is low in nutritional value and should only be used to settle an upset tummy.

Supplements – If you plan on feeding your Shorkie only homemade food, you will need to supplement his diet with calcium. Another reason to use supplements is if the dog food is frozen before being eaten by your dog, many nutrients are lost when food is frozen. Follow instructions on the packaging for the correct amount to add for your dog's weight, age and size. Other supplements you might consider adding to his meals are: omega fatty acids and a multivitamin.

A Basic Recipe for Homemade Dog Food

This following recipe is simply a guideline, which you can adapt to your dog's preferences. It makes approximately four cups of dog food.

- 1 pound of chicken or beef, without fat, skin or bones (cut into small pieces)
- 4 oz. liver, chopped
- 1 medium, steamed sweet potato, chopped
- ½ cup steamed green beans, chopped
- 1 cup of cooked quinoa
- 1 cup of spinach, blended with a cup of water
- 1 Tbsp. coconut oil

1. Sauté the chopped meat and liver in the coconut oil in a pot until cooked through.
2. Add the rest of the ingredients and let simmer for about 10 minutes.
3. Let cool and serve.
4. Store the leftovers in the fridge for maximum of 5 days.

Weight Monitoring

A recent study showed almost 60% of dogs in the U.S. are considered overweight or obese. Unfortunately, the majority of pet owners do not even realize their dog is overweight. Obesity is one of the greatest threats to your dog's long-term health and should not be ignored.

A recent study by the University of Liverpool discovered an overweight dog's life is two to three years shorter than a dog with a healthy body weight. Excess weight can cause arthritis due to the extra pressure on the joints and often suffer from other mobility issues, which affect the quality of your dog's life. Obesity can predispose your Shorkie to a long list of maladies such as: heart disease, diabetes, kidney disease, certain cancers, pancreatitis and bladder stones, to name a few.

Maintaining your dog's healthy weight should be your priority because health complications will be reduced as he gets older. Plus, maintaining a healthy weight will prevent those veterinarian bills from piling up.

How you can tell if your dog is overweight:

- **Feel around your Shorkie's ribs and spine;** you should be able to feel both body parts under a light layer of fat. If you have a hard time finding the ribs, then your dog is overweight. During your dog's annual veterinarian check-up, ask the vet to evaluate your dog's weight. Once your pooch reaches maturity, your vet will determine his optimal weight.

- Your Shorkie should have a visible waistline when viewed from above, but it should not be too prominent. When viewed from the side, your dog's tummy should tuck in and under the ribs and not hang down towards the floor.

- Keep your pooch's weight under control by checking his weight monthly. Place your dog on the scale to get his exact weight. If he is skittish, weigh yourself first then step on the scale with your pup - the difference between the two weights is the actual weight of your Shorkie. Always use the same scale and keep track of each of your dog's weigh-ins.

Your Shorkie's genetic background makes him susceptible to weight gain. While the Shih Tzu is prone to obesity, the Yorkshire Terrier is a typically a slim dog.

Often the reason for your Shorkie's weight gain has nothing to do with his genetics but has to do with you - the owner. It probably is not your dog's daily food that is causing his weight gain but those treats and snacks you give him throughout the day. Even though those treats look small, each one has three to five calories, which add up quickly.

Factors related to weight gain include the following:
- Over-eating, consuming more calories than burning off
- Lack of exercise
- Genetics
- Age
- Neuter/spay status
- Health issues, such as diabetes or hypothyroidism

During your pup's first eighteen months, he will have a fast metabolism, which requires more calories for burning. On the other hand, a full-grown Shorkie will weigh between six to thirteen pounds and will requires approximately 200 to 400 calories each day. Small breeds burn about forty calories per pound of body weight each day. If your Shorkie weighs ten pounds, expect to feed him 400 calories each day.

Be sure to follow the instructions on the dog food package to avoid overfeeding. Feed your dog according to his ideal weight for his age and his size. If your dog is obese, slowly reduce the amount of food you were giving him to the correct amount for his ideal weight. Before beginning any type of weight loss program for your Shorkie, be sure to discuss the details with your veterinarian.

Puppies are different... puppies go through rapid growth spurts, meaning their caloric intake can vary. Make sure you do weigh-ins every two weeks to make sure you are feeding your pooch enough food daily to reach his nutritional requirements so he grows into a healthy, happy Shorkie.

If your puppy is overweight, it will impact his bones and joints and cause bone issues, such as hip dysplasia or arthritis, when he is an adult. Unusual weight loss in puppies could be a sign of a health issue that should be addressed by your veterinarian.

Senior dogs are another category to monitor; they can lose weight due to muscle loss caused from a lack of physical activity. However, the majority of senior dogs tend to gain weight, perhaps due to the fact they are slowing down. Less physical activity means fewer calories being burned. It is important to adapt your senior dog's dietary allowance to his lack of exercise.

Before dismissing your dog's slower pace as a result of getting older, make sure there is not an underlying cause, such as pain. Older dogs still need exercise, especially if he is suffering from arthritis, as exercise helps to loosen up those stiff muscles and joints. Senior dogs benefit from a high-fiber diet as it keeps them full longer and maintains a healthy digestive system.

CHAPTER 11
Grooming your Shorkie

Grooming involves so much more than simply giving your Shorkie a bath or taking him to get groomed. Grooming keeps your dog squeaky clean, reduces shedding and most importantly, keeps him healthy.

Brushing

HELPFUL TIP
Best Brush

With their long coats, Shorkies require frequent brushing to avoid tangles and knots. It's recommended to comb your Shorkie's coat before brushing, preferably using a two-level steel comb. After combing, you'll want to brush. The best brush for this type of coat is a pin brush with comfort tips.

Your Shorkie has a long, silky coat, which means he will need to be brushed every day to maintain a healthy coat. Daily, you will need to remove tangles using a slicker brush. Once the tangles are completely removed you can move on to brush your dog's coat using a bristle brush. If matting is an issue, try clipping off the tangles without getting too close to your dog's skin.

If you have a hard time remembering to brush your Shorkie every day, place his brushes in a place where you will see them, such as beside the television remote or near your reading glasses.

Shedding is normal for all dogs, and your Shorkie is no exception. Excessive shedding can be prevented with a wholesome and balanced diet, plenty of exercise and lots of fresh air. However, if you notice extreme hair loss, the cause might be one of the following factors:

- Parasites, such as mites, fleas or lice
- A fungal or bacterial infection, such as ringworm
- Cancer or immune disorders such as thyroid or adrenal diseases
- Food related-allergies
- Stress or anxiety
- Pregnancy or lactation
- Sarcoptic mange
- Hot spots

CHAPTER 11 Grooming your Shorkie

One of the advantages to brushing your Shorkie daily is you will consistently be making sure his skin is healthy. For example, if you notice any unknown sores, lumps, rashes or scabs, you should consult with your veterinarian. The same is true if you notice any patches of dry, brittle hair that falls out easily.

Photo Courtesy of Jody Rocca

Bathing

You should bathe your Shorkie at least once every three months, but he might require more frequent baths if he has skin problems or spends more time outside.

The following steps are everything you need to know to keep your dog looking and smelling his best:

1. Before your Shorkie's bath, be sure to brush out excess dead hair and remove any mats. Place him in a tub or basin filled with approximately four inches of lukewarm water.

Photo Courtesy of Stephanie Grammer

CHAPTER 11   Grooming your Shorkie

2. Either use a spray hose or a large pitcher to thoroughly wet your dog.
3. Avoid getting water in your dog's eyes, ears or nose. Use a damp wash cloth to remove any debris or dirt.
4. Once your pooch is completely wet, gently massage the dog-formulated shampoo into his coat. Start from his head down to his tail. Rinse and repeat if needed.
5. Take your dog out of the tub and dry him off with a large towel by rubbing him dry.

If your Shorkie thinks bath time is playtime, try putting a floating toy inside of the tub or basin to distract him. Human shampoo is not toxic for your Shorkie, but it does contain fragrances that could irritate his skin.

Nail Clipping

If you notice your Shorkie's nails are clicking against the floor while he walks or are getting snagged on the carpet, then it is time for a trim. Urban dogs who walk on rough pavement might only need their nails cut once a month. On the other hand, rural dogs might need weekly pedicures.

There are two different types of nail clippers - a scissor-type or guillotine. Both styles work well so choose the design you feel the most comfortable using. Another option is a nail grinder to sand the nails down but the loud noise and the vibrations can frighten some dogs.

Most dogs are squeamish about getting their feet touched, which is why you should get your pooch used to having his feet touched while he is still a puppy.

Start by rubbing your hands up and down your dog's legs, gently pressing down in between his toes each time. Do not forget to give him lots of praise and rewards each time he allows you to do this. After two weeks of daily foot massages, your Shorkie should be ready for his nail clipping. This method works well if your older Shorkie is ticklish or wary about having his feet touched.

Before clipping your dog's nails, be sure to give him a vigorous workout and ask a family member to help you.

How to trim your Shorkie's nails:

1. Firmly but gently, hold your dog's paw in your hand and spread out each toe. Hold the nail clipper at a slight angle, cut from the top to the bottom. Cut off the tip of the nail without giving it a blunt angle and maintain the natural curvature.

2. Inside the nail you can see a white-colored circle - this is the nail quick. The quick is the vein that runs into the nail from his paw. Avoid cutting too close to the quick as it will be quite painful for your dog and may bleed. If your Shorkie has darker-colored nails, you will need to be extra careful cutting his nails because it is difficult to see the quick with a dark nail.
3. Once you are finished clipping his nails, reward and praise his good behavior. If he lets you, use an emery board to smooth out any rough edges.

If you accidently cut your Shorkie's quick, he will probably yelp and struggle to get away. It would be best to stop the nail clipping session, but before you let him go, apply corn starch or styptic powder to the wound. Press the powder into the wound until it sticks, causing the bleeding to stop.

If your dog shows aggressive behavior while getting his nails trimmed or if you have a hard time keeping your hands steady, feel free to ask the groomer to clip his nails for you.

Importance of Good Dental Care

Regularly brushing your Shorkie's teeth can go a long way in preventing bacteria and plaque build-up on his teeth. Plaque hardens into tartar, which causes gingivitis, receding gums and even tooth loss. Treating dental issues in small dogs can be quite traumatic as they will need to be anesthetized for the procedure. So, it is best to prevent them from the start.

How to clean your Shorkie's teeth:
1. Get your Shorkie used to having his teeth brushed. Gently massage around his mouth for about thirty to sixty seconds daily for about two weeks. Once he is comfortable with you touching the area around his mouth, do the same procedure daily but to his teeth and gums.
2. Place a small amount of dog-formulated toothpaste on your finger, let your Shorkie smell it first, and gently massage it onto his gums; this will, get him used to the texture and the taste.
3. Next, introduce the toothpaste on the dog-formulated toothbrush. Often, the toothpaste will have soft, plastic bristles. Another option is a toothbrush that is designed to slip over your finger, which allows you to slowly massage you dog's gums.
4. Place the brush at a 45-degree angle and use small, circular motions to clean your dog's teeth and gums. Work on one spot at a time until your Shorkie gets used to the feel of the toothbrush inside of his mouth. Pay extra attention to the back teeth, which tend to build-up more tartar.

5. Once you get your technique down, brush your dog's teeth two to three times a week. If you stop brushing his teeth for a few months, you probably will have to familiarize him with the procedure once again by starting fresh.

Never use human toothpaste with your dog as it contains ingredients that can irritate your pup's tummy. Instead, look for a toothpaste especially designed for smaller dogs like Shorkies. Often dog toothpaste comes in different flavors, such as chicken or beef.

Oral disease in Shorkies can manifest itself in different ways. So, once a week, lift your dog's lips and examine his gums; they should be pink not white or red and there should be no signs of swelling around the teeth. Your Shorkie's teeth should look clean and white, with no signs of brownish tartar build-up. If you notice your dog's gums are inflamed, make an appointment with the veterinarian to examine him. Other signs of oral disease include, drooling, loose teeth, cysts under the tongue or inflamed gums.

Dog's breath is not particularly fresh smelling to begin with! Bad breath is one of the first indications your pooch has dental issues. Smaller dogs, like the Shorkie are prone to plaque and tartar build-up. If plaque is the culprit behind your dog's bad breath, he might need a professional cleaning.

By being familiar with the following common mouth issues, you will be able to determine if it is time to take your Shorkie to see the vet:

- **Periodontal disease** - A gum infection that often results in tooth loss and a risk of spreading the infection throughout the rest of the body. Watch out for bad breath, loose teeth, mouth pain and nasal discharge.
- **Gingivitis** - An accumulation of plaque, bacteria and tartar around the gum line leads to gingivitis. Signs are bleeding, swollen gums and bad breath. Luckily, it can easily be cleared up with regular brushing.
- **Mouth tumors** – Mouth tumors appear as lumps on the gums. They can be quite painful and irritating for your dog while eating. Mouth tumors will need to be surgically removed by a vet.
- **Salivary cysts** – These are fluid-filled blisters located under your dog's tongue or the corners of his mouth. They will need to be professionally drained and often the saliva gland will have to be surgically removed.
- **Proliferating gum disease** – This occurs when the gum line grows over the dog's teeth, which may cause gum infection. Good news is it can easily be treated with antibiotics.

There are other ways to prevent dental problems, such as specially formulated treats that keep your Shorkie's teeth clean and healthy. Certain dry kibble is designed to slow down the buildup of tartar and plaque. Another great option to help keep your pup's teeth strong is by giving him a chew toy to gnaw.

Paws

Keep your Shorkie's paws in tip-top shape by regularly checking them for pebbles, splinters or any other debris. Carefully remove any splinters using a pair of tweezers and keep the hair trimmed in between the toes, which could become matted.

Use a good quality, dog-formulated paw moisturizer on his feet. Avoid using human creams and lotions as they could soften your dog's pads too much, making them prone to injury. Give your pooch a paw massage by rubbing between the pads of his feet and between each toe.

Winter paws – During the colder seasons your Shorkie's paws can chap or crack due to the bitter cold. Rock salt and other ice-melting chemicals could cause your pooch's paws to have painful sores or blisters. Also, the toxic chemicals used to melt the ice could be ingested by your Shorkie when he licks his paws. After coming in the house from a walk, wash your dog's paws in warm water to remove any excess salt or chemicals.

Summer paws – During the warmer months, your Shorkie will be walking on his bare feet on the hot sand or pavement. It is best to walk during cooler times of the day, like the morning or the evening, but even then, your pup's paws can easily become chapped, burned, chaffed or cracked. If he has a blister or red, swollen paws, be sure to wash them in an antibacterial rinse and to moisturize them. For more serious burns, consult your vet immediately.

Ears

Your Shorkie's grooming routine needs to include regular ear check-ups. This is especially important for small dogs, such as Shorkies, as they tend to have excessive ear wax build-up. Never insert anything in your dog's ear such as a Q-tip, because it could cause an infection or trauma. Another warning, don't clean your dog's ears too often, or they could become irritated.

How to clean your Shorkie's ears:

1. If your Shorkie's ears appear to be dirty, use a small piece of gauze or a cotton ball dampened in mineral oil or a liquid ear cleaner formulated for dogs,
2. Gently fold back your dog's ear and carefully wipe away any ear wax or debris you can see.
3. Instead of rubbing at the ear to remove the debris or ear wax, gently wipe it.

All dog breeds are susceptible to ear infections, as water or debris can easily become lodged inside of the ear.

Regularly check your Shorkie's ears for any of the following symptoms:
- Ear scratching or wiping his ears on the floor or against the furniture
- Odor radianting from the ear
- Brown or yellow discharge
- Redness and swelling
- Scabby skin around the ear flap
- Loss of balance
- Hearing loss
- Excessively shaking his head or tilting it to the side

If you notice a brownish or black build-up of earwax (looks like coffee grounds) in your Shorkie's ear, he could have microscopic ear mites. Be sure to make an appointment with your vet as soon as possible.

Eyes

Check your Shorkie's eyes monthly for potential symptoms, such as tearing, inflammation or cloudiness. Place your dog in a brightly lit area of the house, preferably natural light, and look into his eyes. Your pup's eyes should be bright and clear, and the area surrounding the pupil should be white not yellow. His pupils should be alert and equal size, with no discharge on the corner of his eyes. Using your thumb, gently pull down your Shorkie's lower eyelid to see the inner lining; it should be a pale pink color and not red or white.

On a daily basis use a clean, damp cotton ball to wipe any gunk away from your Shorkie's eyes. Being careful not to touch his eyeball. If your pooch is constantly suffering from running eyes or from a discharge, consult your vet as your dog might have a clogged tear duct or an eye infection.

The following symptoms are clear indications your dog might have an eye infection:
- Crusty gunk and discharge around the corner of his eyes
- Teary eyes and tear-stained fur around the eye-socket
- Cloudiness
- Swollen eyelid
- Unequal pupil size
- No desire to open his eyes

Keep the hair around your Shorkie's eyes trimmed as long hair can cause eye damage if it accidently pokes or scratches his pupils. Wind or air conditioners will dry out your dog's eyes, causing irritation and possibly infection.

Professional Grooming

Grooming your Shorkie is an excellent opportunity to bond with your dog. However, professional grooming can be a time and energy saver. Plus, your dog deserves to be pampered!

There are both advantages and disadvantages to taking your dog to a professional groomer…, here are the details:

Pros…
- Groomers have years of experience and can do the job in less time than you.
- Groomers use professional equipment and tools, ensuring a top-notch job.
- They provide specialized treatments, which address de-shedding and ringworm.
- They also do a quick, medical exam, such as checking and cleaning your dog's anal glands and ears.
- Often, groomers include a nail trimming.

Cons…
- The cost can add up, especially if your dog needs to get groomed every six weeks.
- Some dogs suffer from anxiety and stress simply from being left at the groomer for two or three hours.
- It takes time to find the right groomer for you and your Shorkie

In the end, the decision to use a professional groomer or not depends on your personal preferences and situation. Ask yourself if you have the time and patience to groom your Shorkie yourself or if you can financially afford to send him regularly to the groomer.

Some dog owners prefer combining both methods to save money and to gain experience in learning to groom their dog themselves. For example, they will get their Shorkie professionally groomed once every three to four months, and in between times they will do some minor grooming touch-ups and baths themselves.

Finding a reputable groomer takes time and research. Begin by asking friends and family for any recommendations in your area. Once you

CHAPTER 11 Grooming your Shorkie

have narrowed your options to a few groomers, there are some questions you might want to ask the potential groomer. The questions below are only a guideline. Feel free to ask any other questions that concern you and your Shorkie.

Can I see your facility?
The facility should be clean, modern and well-ventilated. The wash tubs and tables should be sturdy. As you look around, ask yourself if you feel comfortable leaving your Shorkie there?

Do they have liability insurance?
If the groomer is a registered business in your locality, it will have liability insurance. This will give you peace of mind if your dog has an unfortunate accident in the groomer's care. Then, any medical expenses incurred will be covered.

What is the total grooming cost?
Groomers often charge differently depending on the dog's size, coat, and temperament. Ask what services are included. Often, a professional grooming will include a bath, shampoo, haircut, nail clipping and drying.

What type of pet-friendly products do they use?
A general rule of thumb is to look for products that are gentle, high-quality and pet-friendly. Their shampoos and conditioners should not contain any harsh, abrasive chemicals.

What type of training have they received?
Most groomers have been professionally trained through apprenticeships or have attended pet grooming classes. Ask the groomer how long they have been professionally grooming dogs.

Photo Courtesy of Heather Davidson

CHAPTER 12
Preventive Medical Care

You have the privilege of caring for your Shorkie, which involves keeping him safe and healthy. Get the facts about vaccines, parasites and even alternative medical treatments.

Photo Courtesy of Melissa Filek

CHAPTER 12 Preventive Medical Care

Choosing a Veterinarian

One of the most important decisions you will make is choosing a trustworthy veterinarian for your Shorkie. Selecting a health-care provider for your dog is a very personal decision, but you will want to look for a practice that excels in providing the highest standard of care.

When looking for a reputable veterinarian, begin by asking friends, family and trusted neighbors for recommendations. On the American Animal Hospital Association (AAHA) website, you will find a list of accredited veterinarians in your locality as well as an evaluation of the facility, staff, patient care and equipment.

When selecting a vet for your Shorkie, take your time to arrange a meet-and-greet with the veterinarian and to get a feel for the facility. The facility should be clean and well-organized and the equipment should be modern. Vets appreciate when pet owners are interested in their pet's health and well-being.

The following are some questions you should ask when interviewing a vet:

- Is the facility AAHA accredited?
- How do they monitor overnight patients?
- Does the clinic refer patients to specialists?
- How do they evaluate patients requiring surgery or anesthesia?
- Are all of the veterinary technicians licensed to practice on animals in your state?
- What is their protocol regarding pain management?

The above questions are only a guide so feel free to ask any other questions that concern you and your Shorkie's health.

If you have problems with your vet, do not hesitate to switch facilities. Veterinary clinics expect clients to come and go. However, before you depart, be sure to request a complete copy of your Shorkie's medical file. You can ask that your dog's health records be faxed or mailed to either you or the new vet.

Microchipping

More than eight million pets end up in shelters across America each year, and only 15% to 20% of them are reclaimed by their owners. One of the best ways to ensure you can find your lost dog is by having him microchipped.

> **HELPFUL TIP**
> **Identifying Glaucoma**
>
> Shorkies may be slightly more likely to develop glaucoma than other breeds. Glaucoma is a disease of the eyes that results in increased pressure in the eyes. This increased pressure can cause degenerative issues to occur in the optic nerve and retina. Here are some signs that your dog may be suffering from glaucoma:
> - Watery discharge from eyes
> - Cloudy eyes
> - Loss of appetite or lethargy
> - Eye pain (can be identified if your dog rubs eyes excessively or recoils from touch near that eye)
>
> If you suspect that your dog may have an issue with their eyes, don't hesitate to speak to your veterinarian!

Microchipping is a tiny chip that is inserted under your pup's skin, often between his shoulder blades. The microchip has a one-of-kind identification number that can be read by a scanner. Microchipping is becoming more and more popular as it locates your pet if he is lost but if he is stolen.

Generally, the entire process takes only a few seconds or about the time it takes to give your dog an injection. It will take more time for you to fill out all of the paperwork involved than it will to insert the microchip! Microchipping does not necessarily have to be completed by a vet, but it is highly recommended you use a vet's service.

If your dog is squeamish around injections and needles, you might want to consider getting him chipped at the same time he is being neutered. Most pet owners opt to have their pooch chipped when they are spayed or neutered for this very reason. The pain is similar to using a needle to draw blood; some dogs flinch, others do not.

Microchipping costs around $50 if performed alone, but if you combine the procedure with a general check-up, etc., it will cost less because you are already paying for the office visit. Once your dog is chipped, be sure to register his identification number and to keep your account updated with new phone numbers and addresses.

Even though your Shorkie is chipped, he still should wear a collar with tags on it. Most people do not have access to a universal scanner to scan the chip, but they will phone you if your phone number is on your dog's collar. Microchipping is only one part of your pup's identification system.

A microchip will not prevent your dog from accidently being hit by a car, so do not let him run loose.

CHAPTER 12   Preventive Medical Care

Neutering and Spaying

Getting your Shorkie neutered or spayed is one of the most important health-related decisions you will have to make. Both spaying and neutering require minimal hospitalization and offer many health benefits.

Spaying is a veterinary procedure that involves removing a female dog's ovaries and uterus. Here are some reasons why you should consider spaying your female Shorkie:

- Spaying helps to prevent uterine infections and breast cancer. It is recommended to spay your dog before her first heat for optimal protection against these diseases.
- A spayed dog will not go into heat during breeding seasons. Often, an un-spayed female dog in heat will urinate all over the house and yowl loudly trying to attract a mate.
- Spaying prevents unwanted litters.
- If your unsprayed female Shorkie accidently mates with a larger dog, her uterus may be too small to accommodate the litter and could rupture, causing serious injury. Spaying prevents this possibility.

Neutering is a veterinary procedure that involves removing the testicles of a male dog. Here are some reasons why you should consider neutering your male Shorkie:

- Neutering helps prevent testicular cancer.
- Your dog will not roam the neighborhood in search of a mate. An unneutered male dog will do everything in his power to find a mate, including digging a hole under the fence or running across a busy highway.
- A neutered male dog will be much better behaved and less aggressive. Also, he will not have the desire or the need to mark his territory by spraying urine all over your house and backyard.

Neutered and spayed Shorkies are both much better behaved as they will focus their undivided attention on their human family instead of finding a mate. Many aggression issues are eliminated when your pet is neutered or spayed. Contrary to what some people believe, spaying and neutering will not make your Shorkie fat; a lack of exercise and over-eating is what will make your dog fat.

Many states and countries have established low-cost programs for spaying or neutering, which makes surgery an affordable option for all pet owners. If you are not planning on professionally breeding your Shorkie, then you should definitely consider getting your Shorkie neutered or spayed.

Internal Parasites

Most pet owners are aware of external parasites, such as fleas, ticks and lice. However, they do not realize internal parasites are quite common, and they cause serious health issues if not taken care of quickly. In order to protect your Shorkie's health, it is important you familiarize yourself with common internal parasites and how to prevent them.

Some internal parasites reside inside of the dog's gastrointestinal tract, causing havoc with the dog's digestive and immune system. Ideally, it is best to treat the problem before it begins. Deworming is designed to protect your dog from these harmful internal parasites. Discuss a deworming schedule

Photo Courtesy of Juli Marcelli

CHAPTER 12   Preventive Medical Care

for your Shorkie with your vet. Deworming products can either be purchased over the counter or with a prescription from your veterinarian.

Regular check-ups can catch parasites and prevent infections in dogs. Your veterinarian will evaluate a stool sample from your dog once or twice a year, looking for parasites and heartworms. It is more cost efficient to catch the parasites before they start to wreak havoc on your dog's body.

Internal parasites are often transmitted when a dog unknowingly consumes parasite spores or eggs in some contaminated food, fecal matter, water or soil. Some internal parasites, such as hookworms and roundworms, can be transmitted to humans such as hookworms and roundworms. Regular veterinary care and deworming is the best preventive measure for healthy dogs and for pet owners.

Here are some common internal parasites that affect dogs:

Whipworms

Whipworm infections are caused when your dog eats contaminated soil or fecal matter. Common symptoms are bloody diarrhea, weight loss and lack of appetite. Whipworm eggs can live for years in the ground. If your pup has been diagnosed with whipworms, he will need to take a monthly heartworm medication to avoid reinfection. Whipworm infections are commonly treated orally for three days.

Tapeworms

Tapeworms live in the small intestines of their hosts. Dogs can easily become infected when they eat fleas, small rodents or uncooked meat containing an immature form of the worm. Tapeworms can be observed in your dog's stool and look like long, white chains or grains of rice. Humans can be infected by tapeworms, by accidently swallowing a flea. Tapeworm treatments are treated orally or by injection.

Roundworms

Roundworms are very common in dogs. Often, they can be spotted in your dog's stool and look like spaghetti. Other typical symptoms include: a swollen, pot-belly appearance, weight loss and diarrhea. Often, roundworms are passed on to puppies through their mother. Adult dogs might become infected by eating fecal matter, eggs in the soil or contaminated water. Roundworms can easily be treated orally in about three days.

Hookworms

Hookworms are another common internal parasite in dogs, which cause anemia, bloody diarrhea and extreme fatigue. Dogs can be contaminated with this parasite by consuming fecal matter or soil. Also, puppies can be infected while nursing from their mother. Hookworm larvae can burrow in to the skin of your dog. Hookworm infections can easily be treated orally for about three days.

Giardia

Giardia are found in contaminated soil or fecal matter. This internal parasite can cause diarrhea but many dogs are asymptomatic and display no symptoms. Giardia infections are treated orally for a period of three to ten days, as dogs can easily become infected after treatment.

Coccidia

Coccidia lives on your dog's intestinal wall and can cause weight loss, fatigue and bloody diarrhea. Coccidia symptoms are not as severe in adult dogs as they are in puppies. Coccidia infections are treated orally for a period of five to twenty-five days. Often, it is necessary to repeat the treatment three weeks after the first treatment.

Heartworms

The heartworm is a type of parasite that invades your dog's bloodstream and is transmitted through mosquito bites. As these worms grow and produce larvae, they affect the dog's lungs and heart, causing congestive heart failure and eventually death. Heartworms can grow to about fourteen-inches long. If you live in an area prone to mosquitos that carry heartworms, you should keep your Shorkie on heartworm medication year-round.

Heartworms are more common in the southern states, but they have been reported in dogs from all fifty states. All vets highly recommend giving your dog a monthly preventative heartworm medication to prevent heartworms. Some injections also prevent hookworms and roundworms.

Heartworms are treated by a series of injections. The heartworm treatment is not easy on your dog's health or your pocketbook, as it requires several vet visits, x-rays and blood tests, etc. The treatment itself can cause life-threatening blood clots in your dog's lungs. Also, while your dog is receiving treatment, the dead heartworms can clog his arteries causing your dog to go into cardiac failure. All types of physical activity are strictly prohibited during treatment and depending on the damage to your dog's heart, activity might even be permanently forbidden.

Symptoms of internal parasites will vary depending on the type of parasite. If you notice your dog exhibiting any of the following symptoms, take your Shorkie to see the vet immediately:

- Coughing
- Weight loss
- Lethargy
- Hair loss or hot spots
- Diarrhea that lasts longer than twenty-four hours

The best treatment for all of the above internal parasites is prevention. Talk to your Shorkie's vet about which preventative measures are best suited for your dog.

CHAPTER 12 Preventive Medical Care

Ringworm is not a parasite or a worm but a common fungus infection that affects all types of animals, including dogs and humans. Ringworm grows on the outer layer of the dog's skin, hair follicles and in the nails.

Ringworm is easily spread from an infected animal or contaminated object, such as a couch or a bed, to your Shorkie. Ringworm spores responsible for spreading the fungus, can live up to eighteen months. Even though ringworm is not life-threatening, it is extremely contagious. Contact your vet if you notice any of the following symptoms:

- Dry, brittle hair
- Scabby, swollen skin
- Rough and brittle claws
- Circular area of hair loss

Your vet will do a physical exam and diagnostic exam by taking a sample of your dog's hair and skin cells. Once, ringworm is diagnosed, your vet will discuss with you a treatment plan for your Shorkie. Treating ringworm includes the following:

- Oral medications

Photo Courtesy of Lisa Ruttenberg

- Topical ointments
- Environmental decontamination

Environmental decontamination is necessary as the fungal spores can live for over a year on couches, bedding, carpeting, etc. Ringworm is easily passed to humans and is also known by another name - athlete's foot. Toddlers, elderly and those with a compromised immune system are easily susceptible to the fungus.

Fleas and Ticks

Your Shorkie's soft and warm fur is the perfect environment for harboring fleas and ticks. These pesky insects feed on your dog's blood and can cause your dog to have an allergic reaction or a serious illness due to a tick bite. Prevention is your Shorkie's best defense against these pesky insects. However, it is also important for you to recognize any signs or symptoms in case a vet visit is necesary.

Fleas – Fleas are one of the most common types of external parasites that affect house pets. They are wingless insects that feed on blood, they can jump almost three feet and survive in all types of environments. Their lifespan can range anywhere from twelve days to an entire year, and during that time, they can produce millions of babies, which produce even more offspring.

Symptoms your Shorkie has been infested by fleas:
- Flea droppings can be found throughout your dog's coat, especially near his mouth, ears, abdomen and tail. Flea droppings resemble fine pieces of dark dirt or sand.
- Flea eggs, which resemble white grains of sand
- Excessive scratching, biting or licking of his skin
- Hair loss
- Hot spots or scabs
- Allergic dermatitis

Fleas are expert stowaways; they attach themselves to your dog while he is outside for a walk, or they jump from one dog to another. They love warmer temperatures, which is probably why they set-up home on your pooch. If not controlled, your home can quickly become infested with fleas.

Health complications caused by fleas can be overwhelming. Fleas consume approximately fifteen times their body weight in blood each day. If left untreated, flea bites can cause your Shorkie to be anemic, which is more serious for puppies as a lower red blood cell count could be fatal. Some

CHAPTER 12 Preventive Medical Care

Photo Courtesy of Katie Taylor

dogs have an allergic reaction to flea bites, called allergic dermatitis.

If you suspect your dog has fleas, all of your pets will need to be treated, including indoor and outdoor pets. Also, the indoor environment will need to be fumigated. Your veterinarian will be able to confirm your suspicions, and most likely will suggest one or two of the following treatments:

- Oral or topical treatment or shampoo rinse or powder for your dog.
- Thoroughly cleaning your house, including bedding, rugs and upholstery. A severe infestation will require professional help, which means you and all of your pets will have to temporarily evacuate the home.
- If your Shorkie gets re-infested each time he goes into your backyard, you might need to use a special lawn treatment.

Photo Courtesy of Jody Rocca

Flea prevention:
- Wash your Shorkie's bedding at least once a week in hot, soapy water and brush him with a flea comb
- Keep your yard tidy by raking up grass clippings and leaves. Fleas prefer to conceal themselves in dark, moist areas.
- There are many preventive flea-control measures available, either by prescription or over-the-counter. Be aware some OTC medications, such as flea collars, can be carcinogenic to cats and humans. Always consult with your vet first.

Ticks – Ticks belong to the arachnid family and are considered to be a parasite because they feed on the host's blood. Often, the presence of a tick will not even be noticed by a dog's owner. Ticks can transmit a long list of diseases through their bite; however, the disease transmission varies by certain areas and climates. Ask your vet what kinds of ticks are found in your area.

Ticks bury their head into the host skin and dig themselves in as deep as they can fit. Then, they gorge themselves on your dog's blood. Ticks are most active during spring and early summer, and they conceal themselves in bushes and tall grass, while waiting for a warm host to walk by to attach themselves. They prefer to attach themselves around the head, neck, ears and feet but can be found in other places. Ticks can jump from one animal to another.

How to check your Shorkie for ticks:

Ticks are about the size of a pinhead and are not often noticed until they bite your dog and begin to swell up with blood. If you live in an area where ticks are prevalent, be sure to regularly check your dog. Carefully run your fingers through his coat, paying extra attention to warm spots, such as inside of his ears, his feet and his head. Repeat this every time he comes inside from playing outside.

Health complications caused by ticks:
- Blood loss and anemia
- Tick paralysis
- Allergic dermatitis
- Lyme disease – Deer ticks are the primary carrier of Lyme disease, which causes depression, fever, loss of appetite, painful joints and kidney failure and needs to be treated with antibiotics.

If you do find a tick attached to your Shorkie, it is important to be careful when removing it as the tick's blood could infect your dog or you, if you accidently come into contact with it.

Follow these instructions to safely remove the tick:

1. Prepare a glass jar with rubbing alcohol inside; this is where you will place the tick. This allows you to take the tick in for testing at your veterinary clinic. Put on latex gloves and ask a family member to distract your Shorkie while you extract the tick.
2. Using a pair of disinfected tweezers, gently grasp the tick as close as you can to the dog's skin. Pull straight upwards using even pressure and then place the tick into the jar with rubbing alcohol. Do not twist the tick out, as this could leave the head attached inside of the dog or cause the tick to regurgitate infected fluids.
3. Disinfect the bitten area and the tweezers; wash your hands with warm, soapy water afterwards. Monitor the area for the next few weeks for any signs of an infection. If there is a sign of infection, take your Shorkie and the tick which is inside of the jar to the veterinarian for a check-up.

Many products used to treat or to prevent fleas are also useful in killing ticks.

Keep your yard tick free by keeping the grass well-cut and by removing any large weeds that could be hiding places for ticks.

Holistic Alternatives to Conventional Veterinary Medicine

Holistic alternatives to conventional veterinary medicine are gaining popularity as some pet parents shy away from pharmaceutical drugs and invasive medical procedures.

Many drugs and medicines have side effects and some pet owners prefer to opt for a more natural alternative without the risks associated with Western Medicine. Holistic therapies claim to treat medical issues without invasive treatments or medication.

Before considering a holistic or an alternative treatment, be sure to discuss it with your veterinarian. Some vets do not approve of holistic medicine and therapies as they have not been scientifically proved to work. Yet, that does not mean they do not work as most vets are open to discuss different options that might be suitable for your dog.

Holistic medicine includes a wide variety of different types of treatments. All of them have the same philosophy – Treat all aspects of the patient's body and not simply the symptom. Here are a few types of Holistic alternative therapies for dogs:

Acupuncture – This involves inserting fine needles into a specific zone or part of your Shorkie's body to help restore the natural flow of energy or "chi." Holistic health practitioners use this treatment to treat chronic pain or aliments.

Chiropractors – Doctors who give your dog spinal adjustments to hopefully relieve pain.

Herbal treatments – Treatments, such as alfalfa, are used to treat a wide variety of illnesses; for example, allergies and arthritis.

Massages – These are helpful in reducing your dog's stress and anxiety, and at the same time, it will improve his circulation and relieve pain.

Nutritional supplements – These are used to make up for nutritional deficiencies from a homemade, raw diet. Often - they include Omega fatty acids, vitamins and amino acids.

As with any type of treatment, use good judgement when using them. Just because an herbal substance states it is healthy, does not mean it is harmless. Always consult with your veterinarian before starting any type of holistic treatment, including herbs and supplements.

CHAPTER 12 Preventive Medical Care

Vaccinations

Getting your dog vaccinated is one of the best ways to give him a long and healthy life. Your veterinarian can help determine a vaccine regime for your Shorkie taking into consideration his health and lifestyle.

Vaccinations are designed to help the body fight off the organisms that cause disease. Vaccines are made up of antigens, which the immune system identifies as the same disease-ridden organism, but they do not actually cause the disease. When the vaccine is introduced into the body, it prepares the immune system to fight off the real virus in its entirety, and it reduces the side effects of the illness.

Most vets recommend administrating core vaccines to healthy dogs. Core vaccines are common vaccinations against common ailments that affect the majority of canines. Core vaccines include canine parvovirus, canine hepatitis, distemper and rabies. Non-core vaccines are given to the dog by taking into consideration his lifestyle and the dog's exposure risk. Non-core vaccines include borrelia burgdorferi, Bordetella bronchiectasis and Leptospira bacteria.

Photo Courtesy of Reginna Kellogg

Your vet will determine which vaccines are necessary for your Shorkie. Your vet will also determine a vaccination schedule for your pooch, taking into consideration his age, medical history, environment and lifestyle.

Puppies – The puppy's mother will pass on her antibodies while nursing your pup. Puppies will receive a series of core vaccines when they are six to eight weeks of age. A vet will administer a series of three different vaccinations with three to four-week intervals, with the final dose being administered at sixteen-weeks of age.

Adult dogs – Depending on your Shorkie's lifestyle, he might require annual vaccines or booster shots every two to three years.

Each state and country have its own laws regarding the administration of rabies vaccines. Some states require an annual rabies vaccine and others require a rabies vaccine every three years. In the majority of the country, a valid rabies vaccination is mandatory.

Risks associated with vaccines:

Because the vaccination is designed to mildly stimulate your dog's immune system to fight off the actual disease, normally the injection causes mild symptoms of the illness. The stimulation can also cause irritation at the injection site, fever or even a slight allergic reaction.

There are, however, rare cases of more severe symptoms caused from the vaccination. As with any type of medical procedure, there can be complications and risks involved. In most cases from being vaccinated, the risks are few and far between, and the advantages are worth the risk.

The majority of dogs have few side-effects from a vaccine. Reactions are often short-lived and rarely require veterinary care. Here is a list of common reactions:

- Sluggish
- Fever
- Lack of appetite
- Vomiting
- Swelling, pain, redness or hair loss around the injection site
- Seizures
- Difficulty breathing
- Diarrhea

Schedule your Shorkie's vaccinations for a time when you will be able to monitor him during the next following days. If any of the symptoms are severe, such as seizures or lameness, call your vet immediately.

Pet insurance

Currently, more than fifteen different insurance companies in the United States offer pet insurance, but less than 1% of pet owners purchase this insurance.

On average, a dog owner spends approximately $250 per year on routine vet visits. What happens when the unexpected occurs? The cost of veterinary care can quickly add up. For example, a typical corrective surgical procedure, such as cataracts for a senior dog, can cost $1200 and up. Foreign-body ingestion in the small intestine can cost $1700 and up to treat.

The cost of pet insurance:

The price will vary depending on the age of your dog and the type of coverage. On average, most pet insurance premiums cost about $20 to $50 monthly.

Unfortunately, there is no right or wrong answer regarding whether or not you should buy pet insurance for your Shorkie. If you do opt to purchase the coverage, as with all insurance plans, be sure to read the fine print very carefully.

Self-Insuring is another option:

If you feel pet insurance is too expensive, then another option is setting up a savings account for your dog. You can always deposit an established amount into an account on a monthly basis and use it only for extraordinary medical care for your dog. This is an excellent option if you are disciplined with money.

The bottom line – veterinary care can be expensive, especially if your dog needs costly diagnostics, care and treatment. If you do decide to purchase a pet insurance plan, be sure to read every word of the policy and to understand what you are actually getting before you sign.

CHAPTER 13
Caring for a Senior Shorkie

Your senior Shorkie will require different care than when he was younger. Smaller dogs, such as your Shorkie, begin their senior years at around eight or nine of age. By learning to pay attention to how aging affects your dog, you will be able to help him feel comfortable and to age gracefully.

Photo Courtesy of Justine Paduch

CHAPTER 13   Caring for a Senior Shorkie

Physical and Mental Signs of Aging

As your dog begins to age, he may start to show signs of mental and physical aging. While some dogs never show many signs at all, it is possible your four-pawed companion will begin to slow down, gain weight more easily and have a harder time standing up.

Poor vision – If you notice your dog's eyes are cloudy, it might be an indication of cataracts, glaucoma or other eye diseases. If you notice your Shorkie is bumping into things or has difficulty recognizing familiar people or objects, he might have vision loss. Consult with your vet, and they can do an eye exam to be sure.

> **HELPFUL TIP**
> **Preventing Tooth Loss**
>
> Shorkies may be prone to tooth decay as older dogs due to genetic factors passed down from their parent dog breeds. To help prevent this, it's important to take your dog to the vet for regular dental cleanings. At home, you can brush your dog's teeth and offer him chew toys that are designed to clean your dog's teeth.

Hearing loss – Hearing loss in dogs is often a gradual process, so it is difficult for the pet owner to notice the symptoms. Hearing loss is often confused with a behavioral issue referred to as selective hearing. Hearing loss symptoms in elderly dogs may include one or two of the following: being unresponsive when called, difficultly waking up, failure to respond to familiar commands and shaking or tilting his head to the side. If you notice any of the above symptoms, consult with your veterinarian.

Stinky breath – It is common for dogs to have smelly breath at any age. However, if you notice your dog's breath is worse than normal, it could be an indication of gum disease, infection or tooth decay. As your dog ages, his immune system will weaken, making him prone to oral infections. Your vet may recommend a good dental cleaning and some basic blood work to eliminate any concerns about infection. The best prevention for senior dog dental problems, however, is to make sure you start consistently brushing your dog's teeth when he is young.

Struggling to stand or sit down – As your Shorkie ages, he may have trouble climbing stairs and standing or sitting. You might observe your dog's back legs weaken and start to give out under his weight. Your pooch's mobility issues are most likely caused by arthritis. Often your vet will recommend pain medications and supplements - plus an exercise regimen suited for your dog.

Appearance of lumps and bumps – Some senior dogs are prone to developing harmless, fatty lipomas. If you notice any new lumps or bumps growing on your dog's skin, always get it checked out by your veterinarian to rule out the risk of a malignant tumor.

Weight change – Since your senior Shorkie is less active, it is common that he will gain weight. You might have to adjust the quantity of food you feed him and establish an exercise regime to help him maintain a healthy weight. If you notice your dog is losing weight, it might be related to muscle loss from lack of appetite or digestive issues. If your Shorkie loses more than 10% of his total body weight in a few months, consult with your veterinarian.

Bathroom issues – If your Shorkie has difficulty going to the bathroom or has incontinence, it may be a sign of a urinary tract infection or kidney disease. Your vet will prescribe medication for your dog's bathroom issues. Incontinence is common in older dogs who suffer from dementia as they begin to forget their housetraining.

As your Shorkie ages, physical changes are not the only differences you will observe. Often, behavioral issues may arise, and they can be an indication of physical problems. For example, if your tenderhearted Shorkie suddenly transforms into Mister Grumpy, he might be in pain caused by arthritis. Or perhaps your hyper-active pooch is suddenly sleeping all day. Senior dogs need more rest than younger dogs, let him sleep.

However, some behavioral changes are caused by canine cognitive dysfunction syndrome (CDDS). Research shows CDDS is similar to Alzheimer's disease and affects about 20% of all dogs over eight years of age. Here are some behavioral changes to watch out for in your Shorkie:

- Fear of familiar objects or people
- Increased vocalization, such as barking, whining or howling
- Incontinence
- Separation anxiety
- Repetitive or obsessive behaviors
- Change in sleep schedule or extreme restlessness or pacing at nighttime
- Confusion and disorientation

If you notice your dog displaying any of these symptoms, make an appointment with your vet as soon as possible. Your vet will ask you some simple questions to help make a diagnosis and to discuss therapeutic options to help your dog deal with CCDS.

Your vet can also aid you in making important decisions about your Shorkie's future needs and requirements.

CHAPTER 13 Caring for a Senior Shorkie

Illness and Injury Prevention

Whether your Shorkie has brittle bones, arthritis or is simply aging in general, he is more susceptible to injuries and illnesses. There are some simple suggestions to help your dog stay comfortable, injury-free and healthy during his golden years.

Common injuries for elderly dogs include strains, pulled ligaments and bruises. You can easily reduce these common injuries by incorporating these strategies into your dog's daily life:

Photo Courtesy of Nanami Montague

Slip proof your home – Hard wood and tile flooring can be very slippery and dangerous for your older Shorkie. Place rugs in areas where your Shorkie spends most of his time, as this will make him feel more sure-footed and secure.

Ramp-up – Stairs, couches and even getting into the car may be a challenge for your old dog as he could easily fall and slip. At your local pet supply store, you can find a variety of ramps to help your Shorkie with these movements.

Fluffy bed – A soft, fluffy bed can go a long way in supporting your Shorkie's old bones and joints. Invest in a doggy bed that has soft sides and will allow your dog to rest his head so he can comfortably observe his surroundings.

Avoid extreme temperatures – Your senior pooch is more sensitive to temperature changes and can easily suffer from frostbite, hypothermia or heatstroke. If the weather outside is extremely hot or cold, keep your Shorkie inside.

Daily exercise regime – Your dog might not have the stamina he used to have, but he still needs regular exercise and mental stimulation. Change his routine by incorporating frequent, shorter strolls around the block. If possible, walk on the grass or a dirt path, as it will be softer on your dog's sore joints than a concrete sidewalk or a blacktop driveway.

Photo Courtesy of Faye McMillan

Weight Issues – As your Shorkie ages, he will move less and burn fewer calories, making him more prone to gain weight. Extra weight puts pressure on your dog's joints and heart, which could lead to health issues. Talk to your vet about recommendations to change your dog's diet.

Take it easy – Your elderly dog will need more time to eat, walk, go to the bathroom, etc. Be patient and give your dog the extra time he needs. Also, your senior Shorkie will love long naps and cuddling on your lap.

Common, Age-Related Illnesses

During your Shorkie's golden years, he may begin to experience one or two of these common age-related illnesses. Since many of these conditions are treatable, be sure to contact your vet immediately if you suspect any of the following maladies:

Hypothyroidism – Hypothyroidism often occurs in older dogs when their thyroid gland begins to become underactive and weak. One of the main indications your Shorkie may have hypothyroidism is unexplained weight gain, no desire to exercise or play, weakness and anxiety. Also, your dog will have itchy skin and dry, brittle hair that easily falls out. Hypothyroidism can easily be treated with prescription medicine from your vet.

Osteoarthritis – Osteoarthritis causes gradual deterioration of the cartilage covering your dog's joints. It causes joint pain and inflammation, making it uncomfortable for your Shorkie to move about freely. The best preventive measure is keeping your Shorkie at a healthy weight as this will prevent excess pressure on his joints. Make sure your dog's diet includes nutrients that support joint health such as omega 3 fatty acids, curcumin, collagen and glucosamine.

Muscle Atrophy – Muscle atrophy is common in senior dogs as they become less active with age. Often, this causes rear leg weakness, limping, ataxia, paw dragging, flabby muscles and weight loss. It can also be caused by joint pain or arthritis, which reduces mobility due to pain and sore muscles. Your vet will diagnosis the cause of your Shorkie's muscle atrophy and will prescribe dietary supplements and a series of physiotherapy treatments.

Cataracts – Cataracts in dogs occur when the eye's lens loses transparency causing the eye to look cloudy. The cataract prevents light from passing through the lens, which prevents clear vision. The majority of senior dogs with cataracts do not go completely blind, and they adjust very well to their vision loss. Cataracts can be caused by trauma, genetics, diabetes or side effects from certain medications. Your vet will diagnose the cause of the cataract before helping you come up with a treatment plan.

Lenticular Sclerosis – Often confused with cataracts as it causes the elderly dog's eyes to form a white, cloudy reflection, lenticular Sclerosis does not cause notable vision loss. However, if you notice that your senior Shorkie's eyes are cloudy toward the center of his eyes, be sure to get him checked by the vet.

Glaucoma – Your dog's eye is filled with a thick substance called the aqueous humor. Since the eye is constantly producing this jelly-like liquid, this fluid it must constantly be drained; if this does not happen, glaucoma occurs. Glaucoma in dogs has many underlying causes, which will be determined by your vet so he can find the best treatment to help your dog's vision return to normal. If you notice your dog's eye looks swollen, red and cloudy, take him to see your vet as soon as possible.

Grooming

Your senior Shorkie will require extra care with grooming as his skin, coat and even his nails begin to change. For example, due to mobility issues, your pooch might not be able to groom himself as frequently, meaning you might have to brush out his coat more often. Adjusting to your dog's evolving grooming needs need not be complicated or time consuming.

Grooming is an essential part of your dog's health throughout his whole life, and no matter his age, he still needs regular grooming.

However, he needs even more grooming during his senior years. These sessions give you or the groomer an excellent opportunity to note any changes in your dog's overall health. The state of his coat or skin might be an indication of underlying medical conditions.

Grooming your senior Shorkie also helps him to feel and look younger. Many times, elderly dogs who loved being groomed in their younger years suddenly become reluctant about grooming sessions due to physical discomfort. Your stiff-jointed pooch might suddenly nip at you or his groomer, or he might vocalize his objections by barking or whining. However, at the end of the session, your elderly Shorkie will be prancing around like a puppy!

A warm bath will relieve your dog's sore muscles or itchy spots that he can no longer reach. Plus, your Shorkie will drink up the extra attention, and you know he will love a treat or two. Your dog is never too old to be pampered!

If you decide to take your dog to a professional groomer, avoid using discount services that may neglect your dog. Your senior Shorkie might be dealing with joint pain, arthritis, or inflammation, even muscle weakness. Not every groomer has the abilities to handle your old dog's aches and pains so choose carefully.

Whether you decide to groom your elderly Shorkie at home or take him to a professional groomer, here are some tips that need your attention:

Keep sessions short – Lengthy grooming sessions can cause your elderly pooch unnecessary discomfort, pain and stress. An easy solution to this problem is to schedule multiple grooming sessions instead of one long one. For example, plan for a trim and brushing one day and schedule a bath for the following week.

Pay attention to any signs of discomfort – Your older Shorkie may bark, growl, whimper, shiver or squirm if he is uncomfortable during the grooming process. If you, or the groomer notice your dog is not comfortable, stop grooming immediately and let him take a rest or find a more comfortable position. If your Shorkie becomes agitated or frantic, stop the session and continue another day.

Recognize limitations – As your dog ages, his skin becomes thinner and is prone to bruising and tearing, so he may need a medicated shampoo for skin conditions. If your Shorkie has poor eyesight, clipping close to his face might cause anxiety. Or, if your dog has fatty benign tumors or pressure sores you might not be able to get his coat clipped as short as normal.

If you decide to groom your elderly Shorkie at home, be sure to review the detailed instructions in Chapter 11 of this book and take into consideration the following suggestions to adapt the process to your older dog's needs:

Bathing – Place a non-skid mat in the bottom of the tub or basin to help secure your dog's footing when giving him a bath. The water should be warm enough that your dog is not shivering during the bath. Use a specially formulated shampoo for elderly dogs. Thoroughly rinse the shampoo out of your dog's coat.

After the bath, dry your Shorkie using towels and let him give himself a good shake before you start using the hair dryer. Only use the "cool" setting on your hair dryer to dry off your dog. Be sure to get your dog as dry as possible, as water trapped in his coat can cause hot spots or other skin conditions.

Brushing – Make sure all of your dog's brushes and combs are in good condition. Discard any brushes with bent bristles, as the damaged bristles could scratch your senior dog's delicate skin.

Your Shorkie may suffer from a lack of mobility caused by joint pain or arthritis, making it difficult for him to stand in place for long periods. If so, let your dog lie on his side while brushing; then let him switch sides, so you can effectively brush the other side. As you are brushing your Shorkie, look-out for any new bumps, lumps or warts. Even though these are common signs of aging, they could merit a trip to the veterinarian, if they look suspicious.

Nail trimming – An older dog will need his nails trimmed more frequently than a younger dog as he will not be walking as much. Maintaining healthy nail lengths is important as the nail length affects posture. Nails that are too long will cause your dog to torque his spine, which may cause discomfort and injury.

Sanitary areas – As your Shorkie ages, mobility issues will prevent him from cleaning his groin area, so he may require some extra help in that department from you. Keep your dog's groin area neatly trimmed to keep any urine or fecal matter from getting stuck. Also, be aware younger dogs automictically express their anal glands when they defecate, but your senior Shorkie might need your help to express his glands. Talk to your vet if this is a concern.

Nutrition Needs

Without a doubt, nutrition is a vital part of helping your senior Shorkie stay healthy throughout his golden years. However, switching his adult dog food for a bag of senior dog food is not quite enough. While protein, fiber, caloric intake and supplement requirements differ from dog to dog, there are some basics to help you give your elderly dog a nutritious diet.

Caloric intake

As your Shorkie ages, he becomes less active than during his younger years. This means fewer calories are being burned off. Another factor is his metabolic rate begins to slow down, causing excess calories to be stored as fat. Recent research shows senior dogs require 20% fewer calories than an adult dog in order to maintain a healthy weight.

Even though your dog will require fewer calories, he will still need a premium diet that provides all of the nutrients required for him to stay healthy. Studies have recently discovered foods rich in L-carnitine, such as red meats, chicken, fish and dairy products, help your dog's body burn-off stored fat for energy.

Genetics also play an important role in your dog's weight. Some dogs, like people, tend to gain weight while others never seem to gain an ounce. Your elderly dog may eventually stop gaining weight and could actually start losing weight. In this case, your Shorkie will require even more calories to stay healthy, so you will need to give him a diet rich in fat, proteins and calories.

Protein

Protein is essential for your senior Shorkie. Even though your dog still may be leading an active lifestyle, as he ages, he will begin to lose muscle mass. In layman terms, this means your dog's protein reserve is being depleted, causing the immune system to weaken. As the immune system weakens, so does your dog's ability to respond to stress, infections or physical trauma.

If your dog does not have enough protein reserves, his body will deplete its reserves of amino acids used for repairing muscle tissue and providing energy. A typical senior dog food should provide 25 to 30% of the calories derived from proteins. Avoid dog foods that contain fillers; instead choose foods with protein-rich foods, such as lean red meats, chicken, fish and dairy products.

Fiber
Fiber is useful in helping your Shorkie lose weight, if needed. However, certain cellulose-based fibers are difficult for your dog to digest and might prevent nutrients from being absorbed. Avoid dog foods that contain bran flakes, psyllium husks, and dried peas.

Fiber is useful in alleviating constipation, which is a common issue for elderly dogs. Another advantage to fiber is it can help control your senior Shorkie's blood sugar levels. Research has discovered soluble fibers help dogs absorb nutrients more efficiently and regulate glucose levels. Some good, soluble fibers are sweet potatoes, carrots, brown rice, milled flaxseed, wheatgerm, kale and kelp.

Sodium
Many elderly dogs need to follow a low-sodium diet if they suffer from hypertension, cardiac and kidney problems. Be aware commercial dog food often contains more sodium than required by your dog's daily requirements.

Choosing a Premium Senior Dog Food

At the moment, there are not any official regulations for senior dog foods, which is why you need to educate yourself on how to find a premium-quality dog food for your Shorkie. Unfortunately, not all senior formulas provide the nutritional requirements for an elderly dog.

Here is a list of the nutritional requirements you should look for:
- Contain complex carbohydrates with a low glycemic index like whole grains and vegetables.
- Contain 25 to 30% protein levels from lean red meats, chicken, fish, eggs and dairy products.
- Contain 10 to 15% healthy fats.
- Include omega fatty acids, such as linoleic and alpha-linoleic acids.
- Contain essential minerals and vitamins, such as zinc, copper, selenium, folate and biotin. Also, vitamins A, D, E and K plus complex vitamin B's.

Look for dog foods that are made from quality ingredients, such as human-grade organic red meat and those free of artificial preservatives and chemicals. No matter how healthy your senior dog is, do not add extra strain on his immune system by feeding him a poor-quality, generic dog food, which does not have any nutritional value. Instead, this type of food is full of junk. For example, sugar, chemicals, additives and preservatives.

Overweight senior dogs – If your four-pawed companion is overweight, it is a good idea to look at reducing his caloric intake and to concentrate on muscle-building proteins in the form of red meat, fish and chicken. An overweight dog can develop diabetes, and excessive weight also puts pressure on his joints, which could cause arthritis.

Senior dogs with health conditions – If your elderly Shorkie has health issues, you will want to consult with your veterinarian about the best options for feeding your pooch.

Health issues related to insufficient nutrients in your dog's diet:

- Diabetes: If your dog is diabetic, he will need a diet high in meat-based proteins, moderate levels of fat and fiber and low levels of carbohydrates.
- Liver issues: If your Shorkie has liver problems, he will need a diet based on high-quality, whole proteins with easy-to-digest simple carbohydrates.
- Kidney problems: If your Shorkie has kidney issues, look for a dog food with lower levels of phosphorus. Wet or canned dog food have the lowest levels of phosphorus but be sure to choose a premium quality option for your dog.
- Heart disease: If your dog suffers from heart disease, choose a dog food option low in sodium and fats.
- Arthritis: If your senior dog suffers from creaky, painful joints, then your best option is adding a dietary supplement or feeding him a fresh-food diet.
- Digestive issues: It is normal for an aging dog to have a slower digestive system and extra gas. If your Shorkie suffers from problematic digestive issues, there could be underlying causes, so consult with your vet for the best dietary recommendations.

Fussy eaters – Some dogs lose interest in eating as they age. A simple and nutritious trick to get your pooch interested in eating again is adding a tablespoon or two of homemade bone broth to his kibble. Your Shorkie will gobble up his food instantly. Bone broth is a delicious, nutrient-dense superfood that will positively impact your dog's overall health.

How to make bone broth for your Shorkie:

Bone broth is a nutritious addition to your Shorkie's regular diet. It is a stock made from simmering raw bones for several hours, either in your slow cooker or in a pot on the stove. Bone broth is jam-packed with nutrients and minerals that improve your dog's digestive health, strengthens joints and reinforces his immune system.

Ingredients
- 3 to 4 pounds of raw bones with marrow such as chicken, turkey, rabbit, beef or oxtail
- ¼ cup parsley, chopped
- 2 stalks of celery, chopped
- ¼ cup apple cider vinegar (which helps to pull the marrow and minerals out of the bones)
- 6 quarts of water

1. Place all of the ingredients in your slow cooker or large soup pot.
2. Cook on low heat for 12 hours on the stove on a low simmer or for 24 hours in the slow cooker on low. Add extra water if needed.
3. Allow to cool. Remove the bones, parsley and celery. Discard the bones. Never feed cooked bones to your Shorkie.
4. Once the broth is completely cool, place in the refrigerator overnight. It will form a layer of fat you can skim off and discard.
5. Freeze into smaller portions, unthaw and add a tablespoon or two to your Shorkie's regular food.

Exercise

Just because your Shorkie is slower and less agile than in his younger years does not mean he does not need any exercise. Helping your senior Shorkie to maintain an active lifestyle will prevent common ailments, such as arthritis and muscle atrophy. Even though your dog may not play fetch as fast as he used to, there are still plenty of ways to keep him physically and mentally active. Here are a few suggestions for exercising with your senior Shorkie:

Do...
- Do establish a daily exercise program. The more active your Shorkie is the more agile he will feel. Start off slow and gentle.

- Do take into consideration the climate. Your senior dog does not handle extreme temperatures very well. In the warmer months, take him for walks during the cooler part of the day, and during the winter months, buy your dog a coat.
- Do stick to familiar walking routes. If your Shorkie is losing his hearing or sight, new surroundings may cause your dog to become confused or anxious.
- Do consult with your vet about the amount of exercise your dog is getting. Inquire whether it is enough or too much.

Don't...
- Do not stop walking! Your Shorkie might not be able to go on long walks, but he still will be excited to go for shorter walks. Walking will allow your dog to stretch his legs, sniff out his surroundings and get some fresh air.
- Don't go at your preferred pace... go at your Shorkie's pace. If he needs to lie down while on the walk, then let him rest.
- Don't forget about indoor exercise. If the weather outside is too hot or cold, keep your Shorkie active with some puzzle games.

There are plenty of exercises your senior Shorkie will enjoy, simply remember to go at his pace and stop whenever he looks tired. Here is a brief summary of some age-appropriate exercises for your senior dog:

Walking – Your Shorkie loves to go for walks, despite his age and health issues. Walking is a low-impact exercise that improves his physical and mental health. Grass and sand are preferred walking surfaces for your dog. Avoid asphalt or rough gravel surfaces that could damage your Shorkie's paw pads.

Swimming – If you have access to a lake or dog-friendly pool, then swimming is an excellent exercise during the warmer months. Swimming is a low-impact sport that puts almost zero pressure on the joints, which allows your Shorkie to strengthen his whole body without experiencing discomfort. Many veterinarians recommend swimming as a type of physiotherapy for dogs after major surgeries or injuries.

Some other fantastic exercise ideas include playing fetch in the backyard with your Shorkie, or giving your dog some mental stimulation by playing a game of hide and seek or sniffing games that lead him to a treat. Even, simply letting your elderly dog slowly explore his outside surroundings is an option.

After your Shorkie's workout, give him a gentle massage to soothe his sore muscles. Massaging your dog after exercise can decrease stiffness and alleviate pain, plus it can help to lower his blood pressure and to improve his circulation.

CHAPTER 13   Caring for a Senior Shorkie

How much exercise is too much:

Your dog's exercise tolerance level will depend on his weight, past exercise history and overall health. There are a few ways you can tell if your pooch is pushing past his comfort zone to please you. Here are a few tell-tale signs your pup has reached his physical limit:

- **Excessive drooling or panting:** It is normal for your senior Shorkie to pant while playing outside, but excessive panting and drooling is a sign that he is overheated and dehydrated.
- **Reluctant to play** - If your dog starts slowing down or lying down on the ground while playing, this is a clear indication he is tired and needs to rest.
- **Limping or muscle weakness** - If you notice your Shorkie starts to favor his leg by limping while exercising, stop immediately. If your dog's limp does not improve within twenty-four hours or if it goes away and returns a few days later, take him to see your vet as soon as possible.
- **Coughing or hacking:** If your senior dog is coughing or hacking, it could be a sign of heart or lung issues or Tracheal Collapse, which is common in smaller breeds, such as Shorkies. Repeated hacking can make breathing difficult for your dog, so if he starts to make a honking sound, it is time to stop exercising. If you notice the coughing returns every time he exerts himself, consult with your vet.

Keep a daily exercise journal of how much exercise your Shorkie experiences and adjust his routine if needed. If you notice he is showing signs of discomfort or pain, slow down his exercise program. If you have any questions or concerns, do not hesitate to check in with your vet.

Saying Goodbye

Nothing is more painful than having to say a final goodbye to a pet. There are no words to describe the pain or the sadness. It is so difficult, many pet owners put it off for too long.

Our dogs are our family; we count on them through the good times and the bad. We adore them for their eternal comfort, love and faithfulness. No wonder we try to take our dogs with us wherever we go and may even have a little wardrobe drawer for them!

Your Shorkie has given you a lifetime of memories and surprises that have filled your heart with joy! It is so painful when you see your best friend begin to show signs of aging, weakness or illness. As time passes, you might become increasingly more aware your four-pawed companion is suffering.

When to say goodbye

Some pet owners are lucky as they never have to decide because their dog just passes away peacefully in his sleep. Others will have to make the painful decision about when to put their dog down.

No matter how your dog takes his final breath, when his dear old heart finally decides to go, it will take a piece of your heart along with them.

However, you might notice several actions by your senior Shorkie, which may indicate he is dying:

- **Prolonged lethargy** – A common indication your Shorkie may be dying is he will lie in the same spot for a prolonged period and not show interest in his surroundings or going for walks. If you notice that your Shorkie is lethargic for more than a day or two, it may be a sign it is time to say goodbye to your dog.
- **Stops eating and drinking** – A classic sign there is something wrong with your dog is when he refuses to eat his favorite treats. The lack of thirst and hunger is because your dog's organs are beginning to shut down. If you notice your Shorkie does not want to eat or drink, rule out any health issues first with a quick visit to the veterinarian's office.
- **Lack of coordination** – Another sign your elderly Shorkie may be dying is a loss of motor control; perhaps he may lose balance while standing up or moving around. If possible, keep your Shorkie in a small, confined space without any objects he could knock over or bump into.
- **Incontinence** – When your Shorkie is dying, he will lie in one spot and not even try to stand up to relieve himself. He may also suffer from diarrhea. Keep your Shorkie and his bed clean and dry.
- **Labored breathing** – If your Shorkie has uneven breathing with lengthy gasps for air between inhaling and exhaling, it is a sign he is suffering and is in pain.

If you notice any of the above common, telltale signs your Shorkie is struggling, then you should call your veterinarian immediately.

Your vet will ask you to bring your dog in for a complete examination. She will tell you if there is any chance of your Shorkie recuperating and being healthy again. The vet may recommend treating the issue with medication or a major surgery, but sometimes these options only put off the inevitable.

The bottom line is you should never let your Shorkie suffer unnecessarily. Your best friend trusts you to make the best decision – with only him in mind.

CHAPTER 13 Caring for a Senior Shorkie

How to Say Goodbye:

When the time comes to put your Shorkie to sleep, the best thing you can do for your friend is to be there for him, as he is frightened, scared and in pain. Your pooch needs you to comfort him, telling him how much you love him and are going to miss him. Your face and voice should be the last thing your old friend hears.

Saying that last goodbye to your pup is not going to be easy, but you should focus on remembering your happy memories together. There are a lot of questions and emotions that surround euthanasia, so here are some of the most common concerns:

What will happen when your Shorkie goes to sleep:

Veterinarians have a set of guidelines called "Humane Euthanasia Protocol." These guidelines have to be administrated by the vet whether the euthanasia is performed inside of the veterinary clinic or in the tranquility of your own home.

1. The veterinarian will give your dog a pain tranquilizer; often it will be administered as an injection.
2. Once your Shorkie is relaxed and sedated, the vet will insert an IV to administrate the euthanasia solution.
3. The vet will leave you alone with your dog for a few minutes for your final goodbyes and then return to administer the final drug to stop the heart.

These steps ensure the entire process is painless and stress-free for your Shorkie. The Humane Euthanasia Protocol is the most humane way to put your dog to sleep. However, in the United States, certain counties do not require veterinarians to follow this protocol. Many vets practice a quicker and more affordable method to stop an animal's heart with a single injection of barbiturates.

Barbiturates slow down the dog's central nervous system causing anesthesia and finally death. This type of euthanasia is not considered to be humane as it is not pain-free and causes short-term anxiety and distress. Be sure to insist your veterinarian applies the specific procedure you want used on your dog.

Most often, dogs are euthanized inside the veterinary clinic, but there are vets who are willing to come to your house to put your dog to sleep in his own bed.

Discuss your different options with your vet and ask whether he/she would be willing to make a house call to euthanize your Shorkie. If your vet is not able to make a house call, you may want to look for a mobile veterinarian in your locality. You can find an extensive list of reputable veterinarians throughout the United States and Canada online at the *In-Home Pet Euthanasia Directory*.

Here is a short look at some of the pros and cons of getting your Shorkie put down at home vs. at the clinic.

At-home euthanasia might be the right choice for you if:
- Your Shorkie is too sick to be transported to the veterinary clinic comfortably.
- Car trips or visits to the vet's office cause your dog unnecessary stress and anxiety.
- You feel more comfortable with grieving at home.
- Money isn't an issue, as at-home procedures cost extra.

Photo Courtesy of Michael Fetter & Toniann Christie

CHAPTER 13   Caring for a Senior Shorkie

Vet clinic euthanasia might be the right choice for you if:
- You want your Shorkie's vet to perform the procedure, but she is unable to make house calls.
- You prefer a more neutral location for the procedure.
- Your Shorkie does not get anxious or nervous going for car rides or to the vet's office.
- Your dog is still mobile enough to be comfortably transported in your car.
- Cost is a concern.

Whether you decide on euthanasia at-home or at the vet's clinic, it is a very personal decision, and there are no right or wrong answers. Only you can make this decision.

The cost of clinical euthanasia can cost between $75 to $350 depending on where you live. If you live in a rural area, costs will generally be cheaper than a larger metropolitan area. The cost of at-home euthanasia can cost between $300 to $800. The higher cost might include add-ons and extras.

It is highly recommended you pay for the euthanasia before the procedure as emotions can be running high when the procedure is final, and the last thing you need is to relive the heartbreak by receiving the bill later.

When it is all over, you can request the veterinary clinic dispose of your dog for an extra cost. Some clinics also offer a cremation service or a professional burial service at a pet cemetery.

Now that you have decided when, how and where your Shorkie will be put to sleep, there is still one final question: What do you want to do with his body?

There are two basic options: burials and cremations. Once again, consult with your vet as to what is the best option for you. Your vet will know if there are any city ordinances regarding home burials and if there are any pet-cemeteries or crematoriums in your locality. If you decide on cremation, you can request to have your dog's ashes returned to you in a box or urn.

If permitted in your locality, you can take your Shorkie home and give him a proper funeral he deserves. Bury him in an area you can visit regularly and place some of his favorite items inside of the grave with him.

There is no right or wrong answer to the above choices. You need to decide what will help you keep your Shorkie close to your heart and soul. Take your time to grieve and come to terms with your loss. After all, your beloved pooch was not just a dog - he was part of your family.

If in the future you decide to open up your heart and home to a new dog, never compare your new dog to your "old" Shorkie. Each dog deserves to be loved and cherished for exactly who they are.

www.ingramcontent.com/pod-product-compliance
Lightning Source LLC
Chambersburg PA
CBHW071447070526
44578CB00001B/244